The Psalter for Christian Worship
Revised Edition

The Psalter for Christian Worship
Revised Edition

Michael Morgan

WESTMINSTER
JOHN KNOX PRESS
LOUISVILLE • KENTUCKY

Originally published as *The Psalter for Christian Worship, Revised Edition* in 2010 by Witherspoon Press, Louisville, Kentucky.

2019 edition
Published by Westminster John Knox Press
Louisville, Kentucky

19 20 21 22 23 24 25 26 27 28 —10 9 8 7 6 5 4 3 2 1

Book design by Jeanne Williams
Cover design by Allison Taylor

Library of Congress Cataloging-in-Publication Data
Names: Morgan, Michael, 1948- author.
Title: The Psalter for Christian worship / Michael Morgan.
Description: Revised edition. | Louisville, Kentucky : Westminster John
  Knox Press, 2019. | "Originally published as The Psalter for Christian
  Worship, Revised Edition in 2010 by Witherspoon Press, Louisville,
  Kentucky."
Identifiers: LCCN 2019021674 (print) | LCCN 2019981532 (ebook) | ISBN
  9780664265410 (paperback) | ISBN 9781611649406 (ebook)
Subjects: LCSH: Reformed Church--Liturgy--Texts. | Psalters--Texts.
Classification: LCC BX9427.5.P74 M67 2019 (print) | LCC BX9427.5.P74
  (ebook) | DDC 264/.05137015--dc23
LC record available at https://lccn.loc.gov/2019021674
LC ebook record available at https://lccn.loc.gov/2019981532

Most Westminster John Knox Press books are available at special quantity discounts when purchased in bulk by corporations, organizations, and special-interest groups. For more information, please e-mail SpecialSales @wjkbooks.com.

*To the worshiping communities of
Central Presbyterian Church and
Columbia Theological Seminary,
and to all who would find in these pages
words to frame their prayers and praise.*

Contents

Preface

The psalm paraphrases in this collection were composed during the spring and summer of 1995 for the congregation of Central Presbyterian Church in Atlanta, Georgia.

As part of our congregation's desire to reclaim metrical psalm singing, which is at the heart of our Reformed tradition, Dr. Theodore Wardlaw challenged me to write new Editions of the Lectionary psalms for Eastertide. The worshipers at Central Church have a strong attachment to congregational song, and with their encouragement, I composed settings of all 150 psalms. These psalter hymns were designed to be sung to a variety of tunes that our congregation knew from memory, making them readily accessible.

Never before had I embarked on such a meaningful and self-illuminating devotional exercise. I repeatedly found my life experience reflected in the psalms on which I worked. Often, I would struggle with a particular psalm with little insight or inspiration, and in frustration turn to another, where the words would flow almost as quickly as I could write. Sometimes the first line to come to me would be halfway down the page, and the text would grow from there in both directions until the psalm was complete.

My parameters were defined from the beginning:
1. *Make the texts suitable for congregational singing.* The approach to each text was the same: to condense thought and repetition into single units, paraphrasing those to achieve the sense of the psalm. I sought help in commentaries and devotionals from Calvin and Horne, to Dahood and Brueggemann. Where the Revised Common Lectionary abbreviated the texts or divided the

longer psalms, I considered the same alignment in my edition.

2. *Remain faithful to the character of the psalms.* I have sought not to "Christianize" the psalms, but to balance images and allusions from both sides of the cross (Hebrew poet and the Messiah of the Gospels, the shepherd boy and the Good Shepherd), tempering judgment with justice and vengeance with grace.

3. *Employ modern English language.* In the first edition, a significant number of texts used "thee," "thou," "thy," and "thine" in reference to God. Even though much of our association with the Psalms is cloaked in this classic style, the texts in this revised edition have been reworded in modern English to make them universal in their appeal to those who will sing them.

4 *Commit to the use of inclusive language, both in references to God and to the people of God.*

5. *Provide texts that are suited to a variety of familiar tunes.* The suggested tunes will be found in most standard hymnals. They are suggestions; worship leaders are encouraged to select tunes that may be more familiar to their congregations (being sure that the meter, the accents, and the spirit of the tunes fit the words), or to write tunes of their own.

6. *Make the texts easily accessible as worship resources.* Permission is granted to reprint texts in worship bulletins without having to obtain written permission. All that is requested is acknowledgement of the source.

In addition to the colleagues and friends named in the first edition who generously contributed their scholarship and support, special appreciation for this revision is given to David Gambrell, associate for worship, and Mark Hinds, general editor, with the PC(USA) Office of Theology Worship and Education; and to the worship leaders and congregations who have found in these words new expression for their praise.

Michael Morgan

INTRODUCTION

Metrical psalmody: the name sounds as intimidating and as austere as anything one might associate with staid Scottish Presbyterians! Yet little else is closer to the heart of worship in the Reformed tradition than the psalms of David paraphrased in metered verse. Over four hundred years ago, our first service book, the *Forme of Prayers and Ministration of the Sacraments,* was beloved by the people for the metrical psalter it contained.

We lift up the psalms to God as our prayers. We borrow the language of these ancient texts, and they become our words. We are not secondhand recipients of God's Word, but communicants actively in conversation with God. What seems to set the psalms apart from the rest of Scripture is their sacramental nature, their unique ability to mold and transform the believer.

The psalms we sing and pray may reflect our own sentiments, or may be in conflict with them, but even in conflict, we are able to make them our own prayers. In our praise, they call us to affirm that God creates and sustains us, and deserves more thanksgiving than we can ever express. In our lament, we are assured that this same God will strengthen and nurture and love us.

David Dickson, a Scottish Puritan of the seventeenth century, described the seasons of our lives as a blend of "crosses and sweet comforts." The psalms are reflections of our full human experience, but never without the illumination of who God is, and where we stand in relation to that wonderful Presence.

Christian worship has always included the singing of psalms. Prior to the Reformation, however, liturgical music had gradually become more the possession of the church and less a treasure of the people. In their Latin editions, which few could understand, psalms in worship were sung to plainchant melodies. Gregorian chant may be a pure and expressive means of conveying the prose of the Latin Bible, but it is far less effective with poetry. The use of chant also required most of the service music to be "performed" by trained singers who could read musical notation, while the congregation sang only the simplest responses. As more intricate service music evolved, even these responses became the property of the choir, leaving the people as passive observers of the liturgy.

If liturgical music was to be returned to the people, three things had to be accomplished:

1. Texts had to be cast in the language of the people to be meaningful to those who sang them. The beauty of Latin never made it past the ears of many listeners.
2. Texts had to be cast in a form that people could read, memorize, and assimilate with ease. Short phrases, structured within a variety of rhyme schemes, made texts more comprehensible.
3. A type of music had to be devised that untrained voices could sing, like the simple ballads the people knew by heart and that sustained them through the remainder of the week.

John Calvin's Psalter

John Calvin's innovative psalmody was a fitting solution. Calvin (1509–1564) felt that only those songs given to us by God—the psalms—were worthy to be given back to God. With few exceptions, he desired that only the Psalms of David be sung in worship.

Calvin acknowledged that the psalms would require translation into the vernacular. He also allowed the texts to be rendered in verse. He engaged the poet Clement Marot (c. 1497–1544) and the theologian Theodore de

Bèze (1519–1605) to transform ancient Hebrew verse into the finest French poetry of the day.

English Psalters

The English metrical psalter and the first Scottish psalter found a more humble genesis in the psalm "ballads" composed by Thomas Sternhold (1500–1549), a groom in the chamber of King Henry VIII. Sternhold was no poetic match for Marot, but English-speaking Christians had never sung psalms in their own language, and young Edward, the future king, upon hearing Sternhold singing one of his verses, encouraged him to write more.

Within a few years, both servant and king were dead, and under the violent reign of Mary Tudor, the Church of England renounced many elements of the Reformation. Protestants fled to the Continent. Inspired and informed by the teachings of Calvin, these English Protestants set out to complete a psalter, incorporating the work of Sternhold, but also drawing on the talents of John Hopkins (d. 1570), William Whittingham (1530–1579), William Kethe (d. 1608), and others. The completed "Sternhold and Hopkins" edition, popularly known as the "Old Edition," was published in 1562. In 1564 Scottish refugees, under the leadership of John Knox (1505–1572), published their own edition, in which about a third of the texts differed from Sternhold and Hopkins.

Music found in both psalters came primarily from popular adaptations of some of the new hymns of the Reformation and original tunes contributed primarily by Louis Bourgeois (1510–1561). As a reaction to the complex music of the pre-Reformation Church, the music prescribed by Calvin was in unison so that the congregation might lift a common voice to God without the "clutter" of harmony, counterpoint, or instrumental accompaniment. The wonderful tunes of Bourgeois brought melodic and rhythmic freshness to singing.

Protestants who returned to England during the reign of Queen Elizabeth I brought their psalter. With occasional revision, this translation was retained for more than two hundred years. Competitive metrical editions appeared, most notably the 1612 psalter by Henry Ainsworth (1571–1622) and the 1632 collection by George Wither (1588–1667), but these appealed to the fringes of the Anglican communion rather than to its core. Even the "New Edition" of Nahum Tate (1652–1715) and Nicholas Brady (1659–1726), published in 1696 and revised in 1698 to replace the archaic "Old Edition," met with little enthusiasm. The much-loved verses of Sternhold and Hopkins continued to be sung into the nineteenth century.

Scottish Psalters

Throughout this time, the Scots were in conflict with the English over a variety of matters both political and religious. Queen Mary was put to death by Elizabeth I, who later died with no apparent heir. Elizabeth was succeeded by James I, the son of her Scottish adversary. With the ascent of King James (1603), the Tudor succession ended and the Stuart line began. The two countries were united. The national churches, however, had become too distinct to merge and too entrenched to compromise. From the form of church government and ordering of worship to the form of the psalms they sang, one sought independence and the other sought control.

The final assault by the English Church, led by Archbishop Laud, was to force the Anglican Book of Common Prayer on the Church of Scotland. Appended to this liturgy was a new psalter, attributed to the late King James himself, which Laud believed would make the new service more palatable to the Scots. The plan failed and triggered a civil war with England, which ended with the execution of Charles I and the institution of the Commonwealth under Oliver Cromwell.

The Psalter for Christian Worship

With the new power they were enjoying at the expense of the English, the Scots and the Puritans abrogated the use of the Anglican Prayer Book in favor of their Directory for Worship, and sought to replace the 1564 Scottish Psalter. The Westminster Assembly (1643–1653) examined editions by William Barton (1603–1678), Francis Rous (1579–1659), and others, and in 1650 published its psalter, "more plaine, smooth and agreeable to the Text, than any heretofore." The publication of this edition, known simply as the "Scottish Psalter," delineated English and Scottish psalmody, setting a metrical standard for the Church of Scotland and other English-speaking Presbyterians, which remains virtually unchallenged to this day.

Eighteenth and Nineteenth Centuries

From the beginning of the Reformation, the texts of the Hebrew psalms presented a dilemma for Christians. Many verses in the psalms applied so directly to the experience of the Hebrew people in their struggle or spoke so intimately of the anger and frustration of the psalmist that they were thought unsuitable for Christian song. Further, early metrical settings adhered so strictly to the original Hebrew that twenty or thirty stanzas were required at times to communicate the full psalm text. Restricted to the use of the psalms in worship, such an approach allowed for no proclamation of the gospel through congregational song. Surely praise, thanksgiving, mercy, grace, and redemption were present in the psalms, but the realization of God's covenant through the gift of Jesus Christ was nowhere to be found. The efforts of John Patrick (1632–1695), Isaac Watts (1674–1748), and others brought the psalter into conversation with the New Testament through liberal paraphrases of the original texts.

A second problem remains: the difficulty of producing a metrical edition of the psalms that can be called "poetry" when these texts are to be sung by a congregation at worship. Some of the more "poetic" paraphrases of the psalms, such as those of James Merrick (1720–1769), seem too "sublime" to be confined to the monotony of a long meter or common-meter tune. This may be one more reason that many great poets— George Herbert (1593–1632), John Donne (1572–1631), and John Milton (1608–1674) among them—did not attempt to turn the whole psalter into verse, choosing instead only those psalms that most appealed to them.

The "culprit" in the near demise of metrical psalmody was not the psalms themselves, but performance practice. Since many people could not read music, they depended on a leader, or "precentor," to "line out" the psalms. The tune would be sung, line by line, with the congregation responding, line by line, in echo fashion. So as not to tax the communicants' tonal memories, the psalms were often sung at a snail's pace, with little of the energy Bourgeois had written into his original tunes.

To simplify singing further, only a dozen tunes were allowed for many years, with the hope that congregations would learn them. There are amusing stories of psalm singing in worship where the people sang their favorite tune without regard for the precentor or the rest of the congregation, resulting in what one contemporary critic described as a sound that resembled the bleating of sheep on the moors! Precentors soon began to embellish the psalm tunes with "graces," which so disguised the melodies that congregations were challenged to identify them, much less reproduce them.

In an attempt to salvage metrical psalmody, some presbyteries restricted the singing in worship to choirs composed of parishioners who were willing to learn to sing. Precentors became music educators and offered instruction in singing psalm tunes. Some considered the psalm texts too sacrosanct to be sung outside of worship, however, so "practice verses" were written to be substituted for the psalm when learning the music; these were then discarded at the church door. These texts were personal, secular, and even earthy at times, but singing meant so much to the people that they endured the instruction in order to sing in the choir, and soon some of the choir lofts held more people than the naves.

By the Victorian era and the early twentieth century, psalmody had for the most part been swallowed up in a vast sea of hymns authored by the Wesleys, the poets of the Oxford Movement, and other independent hymn writers.

Contemporary Psalters

As metrical psalms disappeared from regular use in worship, prose settings of the psalms, which had endured in other liturgical traditions, began to take their place. Lectionaries, whether strictly observed or not, regularly included psalms among the lessons. Responsive readings helped maintain the presence of the psalms in worship, albeit in a less than imaginative manner. Those charged with fostering creative and meaningful corporate worship began to seek ways to improve prose psalmody. The ancient practice of antiphonal singing, with repeated phrases sung in response to portions of a psalm, became popular in churches for whom that tradition had long been lost. Congregations could easily learn the refrain and sing "on cue" while the choir changed the psalm verses. These responses or "antiphons" gave the people a means of singing the psalms, though not with the complete involvement that metrical psalmody afforded.

The Christian church is experiencing a time of liturgical renewal, with increased interest in reclaiming traditions and particular practices. One of those traditions is metrical psalmody, as evidenced in the proliferation of psalm settings in many current denominational hymnals. The *Psalter Hymnal* of the

Christian Reformed Church, published and revised continually since 1934; the more recent, original psalters by Christopher Webber and Fred Anderson; and *The Psalter for Christian Worship* have served to provide new and more "singable" metrical editions of the psalms.

A new metrical paraphrase sung to a very familiar tune brings psalm singing closer to the hymnody to which we are accustomed. A well-crafted text, coupled with a tune like "Amazing Grace" or "Hyfrydol," is accessible to any gathering. Familiarity encourages participation, which in turn encourages the whole congregation's active participation in worship.

Through the seasons of life, the psalms offer strength, affirmation, remembrance, and joy. We share these gifts with all generations before us who have known sorrow and gladness, condemnation and redemption, darkness and light, death and resurrection.

May God in endless mercy ever continue to teach us new songs of life in God's presence, providence, and praise.

The Psalms
Book I

Psalm 1

LM (Suggested tunes: CANONBURY; ROCKINGHAM; MARYTON)

How blest are they who venture not
　　Into the dark and sinful way,
But find delight in God's own law,
　　And contemplate it night and day.

As trees beside the stream they grow
　　And flourish, wholesome fruit they bear;
The wicked lot are cast aside
　　And lost to their own dark despair.

The judgment of the Lord is sure
　　And good to those who seek God's face;
The righteous find themselves redeemed,
　　And heirs to God's all-knowing grace.

Psalm 2

8.7.8.7 D (Suggested tunes: EBENEZER; HOLY MANNA)

Why do nations rage together,
    Why in vain do they conspire?
Rulers of earth's vast dominions
    Light the skies with martyrs' fire.
Truth mistaken, God forsaken,
    Banes of righteousness arise;
Yet shall they reap sore displeasure,
    Sure defeat before God's eyes.

To the children of the promise
    God shall give the throne this day;
With a scepter forged of iron,
    They shall dash their foes as clay.
Faith revealing, humbly kneeling,
    Quench the fire and sheathe the sword;
For God's wrath is quickly kindled;
    Blest are they who serve the Lord.

Psalm 3

LM (Suggested tunes: WHEN JESUS WEPT; DEO GRACIAS; ERHALT UNS, HERR)

O Lord, how many are my foes!
  How vast their legions round me press!
From ev'ry side, their threats deride,
  And work to shake my faithfulness.

But You, O Lord, remain my shield,
  My glory and Redeemer still;
I cry to You, who answers me
  Steadfastly from Your holy hill.

My eyes are closed, I sleep in peace,
  Assured that I again will wake;
When arms shall raise, I'll give You praise,
  Rejoicing for Your mercy's sake.

Arise, O Lord, deliver me
  From all who would my life assail;
Your blessing sure will long endure,
  And righteousness at last prevail.

Psalm 4

10.10.9.10 (Suggested tune: SLANE)

God of all righteousness, hear when I pray,
    In my distress be my hope and my stay;
Long I have suffered revilement and shame,
    Great God of mercy, I call on Your name.

Angry, yet silent, I know there will be
    Justice according to holy decree;
Never to answer corruption in kind,
    But in Your promise true peace will I find.

When those around me my faith would confound,
    May I rejoice in Your gifts that abound;
Peace and assurance all discord withstand,
    Safely I rest in the palm of Your hand.

Psalm 5

LM (Suggested tunes: ROCKINGHAM; ERHALT UNS, HERR;
CONDITOR ALME SIDERUM)

O hear the words I speak, my God,
    To my unuttered sighs attend;
And from Your overwhelming throne
    To my frail spirit, grace extend.

For early shall my prayers ascend
    Like incense rising to the sky;
In confidence, I make my plea,
    And in Your faithfulness rely.

Your heart delights in all things good,
    And evil flees if You are there;
Your truth will over pride prevail,
    And justice shall be brought to bear.

But through the bounty of Your love
    Among Your chosen I am cast,
O lead me forth in righteousness,
    And bring me safely home at last.

Psalm 6

7.7.7.7.7.7 (Suggested tunes: REDHEAD 76; DIX; RATISBON)

Lord, rebuke me not in wrath,
  Nor in anger hide Your face;
Vast the heights of agony,
  Great the depths of my disgrace.
Flesh and spirit languish sore,
  O forget my soul no more.

Lord, Your mercies are not bound
  By designs which cannot move,
But are measured in the realm
  Founded through Your steadfast love.
All distress shall pass me by,
  When, by grace, You hear me cry.

Psalm 7

CM (Suggested tunes: MORNING SONG;
ST. AGNES; DETROIT)

O Lord, my God, my refuge sure,
    In You my hope is laid;
Before the looming veil of death,
    My soul is unafraid.

Though failures of my life abound,
    Your mercy shall preserve;
And Your redemptive gift of grace
    Is more than I deserve.

Arise, O Lord, and in Your wrath
    Mete justice swift and smart;
Weigh righteousness against deceit,
    And spare the pure in heart.

For You are yet the sword and shield
    Before whom foes shall bend;
And those whom faith redeems shall sing
    Your praises without end.

Psalm 8

8.6.8.8.6 (Suggested tunes: Rest; Gatescarth)

O Lord, our Lord, Your majesty
   Is sung in all the earth;
Who hung the moon and stars in space,
   And gave to us, Your chosen race,
From dust a noble birth.

How vast the heav'ns, how small are we,
   And yet we feel Your care.
O who are we to own such grace,
   To see Your glory face to face,
Your goodness ev'rywhere?

All creatures bow beneath our feet;
   Through us their wants attend.
For life and love so freely giv'n,
May we preserve the gift of heav'n:
   Earth's love that knows no end!

Psalm 9

6.7.6.7.6.6.6.6 (Suggested tunes: NUN DANKET ALLE GOTT;
WAS FRAG' ICH; O GOTT; DU FROMMER GOTT)

I will give thanks to God,
Who wondrous gifts has given;
My heart delights to praise
The Lord of earth and heaven.
God's justice never fails
To rule with equity;
And measures of God's grace
Are mine to set me free.

Our stronghold sure is God,
Our shelter from oppression;
A constant source of strength
Amid all tribulation.
For those who trust God's name,
Deliv'rance is their prize;
And those who seek God's face
Find favor in God's eyes.

Be gracious, Lord, to me;
How great my desolation;
A saving word from You
My only consolation.
O lift me from the snares
My wicked foes have laid;
And lead me through the mire
Unscathed and unafraid.

Remember, Lord, how we
Your faithful blessings cherish;
Though death may hold us fast,
Our hope shall never perish.
Arise, O God, in might
Against unrighteous hands;
While earth shall fall to dust,
God's kingdom ever stands.

Psalm 10

7.7.7.7 D (Suggested tune: ABERYSTWYTH)

Lord, why stand so far from me?
　　Why desert in time of woe?
Hosts of evil gather 'round,
　　Bait my steps where'er I go.
All ambitions of their hearts
　　Are but for their selfish gain;
Base conceit shall count for naught;
　　Lofty pride resound in vain.

All around, dark shadows fall;
　　Godless hands with swords are raised;
God's great goodness meets with scorn,
　　In its place, injustice praised.
You, O Lord, the Judge of all
　　Shall reward our lives in kind;
Slaves to death, a grave is theirs,
　　Faithful souls, redemption find.

Psalm 11

CMD (Suggested tunes: RESIGNATION;
KINGSFOLD; ELAACOMBE)

The Lord to me a refuge is,
　　When foes my faith deride;
Their fatal schemes I will not dread,
　　If God is at my side.
The sparrow may to mountains flee
　　To dodge the arrow's sting;
I to the Lord will turn for aid,
　　And to God's promise cling.

God's temple is the universe,
　　And heaven's arch a throne;
The good within God's courts rejoice,
　　The wicked die alone.
The Lord delights in righteousness,
　　And crowns pure deeds with grace;
To faithful hearts, with love alive,
　　God turns a smiling face.

Psalm 12

CM (Suggested tunes: LAND OF REST; CRIMOND;
MORNING SONG)

Lord, hear our cry and send us aid,
　　They press from ev'ry side;
The godless bask in vain deceit,
　　And gloat in empty pride.

The words within their hearts are not
　　The thoughts their lips express;
Their lies with honesty supplant,
　　And wrong with righteousness.

As silver cast into the flame,
　　Your promises are pure;
To all who show humility,
　　Rich blessings shall endure.

Psalm 13

7.6.7.6 D (Suggested tunes: LLANGLOFFAN;
PASSION CHORALE)

How long am I forgotten?
   Am I forever spurned?
O keep not from my sorrow
   Your face in anger turned.
My heart is bowed with anguish,
   My foes inflict their pain;
While I no comfort merit;
   No hope for peace regain.

Around me hosts of evil
   Are quick to claim their prize;
If only death could free me,
   I pray You, close my eyes.
But Your great mercy ransoms
   My spirit from the grave;
Not even death can conquer
   God's pow'r to bless and save.

Psalm 14

CM (Suggested tunes: DUNDEE; CAITHNESS; LAND OF REST)

The foolish heart denies the Lord,
　　And mocks divine decree;
The harvest of its work is vain,
　　Its deeds bring misery.

From heav'n God looks upon our hearts
　　To measure good and shame;
The wicked glory in themselves,
　　While we exalt God's name.

They live their evil days as kings,
　　Their scorn brings them to dust;
And from our shackles God will forge
　　A scepter for the just.

Psalm 15

LM (Suggested tunes: GERMANY; WINCHESTER NEW;
CONDITOR ALME SIDERUM)

Lord, who may in Your temple dwell,
    Upon Your holy hill abide?
Those who show love instead of hate,
    Humility in place of pride

A blameless life help me to live,
    Free from contempt and selfish will;
When I through mortal frailness fail,
    God deigns by grace to love me still.

Psalm 16

LM (Suggested tunes: TALLIS' CANON;
CONDITOR ALME SIDERUM; CANONBURY)

Preserve, O Lord, my trusting soul,
   Count me among the saints in light;
May I with them Your mercy gain,
   And rightful favor in Your sight.

How many are their schemes, O Lord,
   Who tempt me from the way I know;
Their gods of gold and strength and thought
   Confront me ev'ry step I go.

You, Lord, are my inheritance;
   Through generations I am heir
To righteousness in place of sin,
   Your grace to save me from despair.

At your right hand I find delight
   In all the blessings kept in store;
The fullness of Your love, my joy;
   I praise Your glory evermore.

Psalm 17

8.7.8.7 (Suggested tunes: CHARLESTOWN;
STUTTGART; RATHBUN)

Hear, O Lord, my plea for justice,
    Listen to my heartfelt prayer;
In Your just deliberation
    May I find redemption there.

Test my heart for its affliction,
    Purify my soul with fire;
Let my mortal tongue speak wisdom,
    Righteousness be my desire.

Keep me, Lord, in sure protection,
    As the apple of Your eye;
Shelter me beneath Your shadow
    When my hour of death draws nigh.

In its wake send vindication;
    To its darkness, show Your face;
Bring me to my resurrection
    Clothed in garments of Your grace.

Psalm 18

CMD (Suggested tunes: FOREST GREEN;
KINGSFOLD; RESIGNATION)

I love the Lord, who is my strength,
    My refuge in distress;
The object of unending praise,
    The source of righteousness.
When bonds of hell encompassed me,
    And death had set its snare;
I raised my tear-filled eyes to God,
    Who heard my plaintive prayer.

The oceans rolled and mountains shook
    At God's unbridled wrath,
And through the blazing holocaust
    God laid for me a path.
While evil foes God judged unfit
    And cast into the flame,
The righteous danced across the coals
    To praise God's holy name.

What god is there except the Lord,
    Whose way is perfect peace;
Whose justice is forever sure,
    Whose love will never cease?
May those who keep their faith in God
    Seek righteousness always;
And to the promise of God's grace
    Respond with songs of praise.

Psalm 19

CMD (Suggested tunes: ELLACOMBE, KINGSFOLD; MATERNA)

The heav'ns unfold Your glory, Lord,
    In ev'ry realm of space,
The outmost bounds of all that is
    Resound Your wondrous grace.
Succeeding days to day confess,
    And nights to night record
In words beyond our sense to hear
    The greatness of the Lord.

The earth's imagined cornerstones
    Acclaim with joy their Source,
Who sets the gleaming stars ablaze,
    And gives the sun its course.
In ev'ry place within the sphere
    Your craft is ever found;
Majestic mountains, seas, and skies
    With ordered might resound.

Your Word is sure and perfect still,
    A source of light and life;
Your Law is right and reason-filled,
    Your peace, the end of strife.
Your everlasting truth and love
    Can scarce be fully told;
More sweet than honey from the comb,
    More precious yet than gold.

You know the secrets of our hearts,
    But deign to love us here;
Preserved from pride and self-conceit,
    We meet You without fear.
May all the words our tongues shall speak
    And all our thoughts in store
Find grace with You, Redeemer, Rock,
    Now and for evermore.

Psalm 20

7.6.7.6 D (Suggested tune: LLANGLOFFAN)

Lord, hear our supplication,
    For trouble is at hand;
And be to us a strong defense
    When foes against us stand.
Remember then our tributes,
    Each sacrifice we bring;
Accept them as Your honor due,
    Our Shepherd and our King.

The Lord shall with a victor's crown
    Adorn the servant's head;
God's foes proclaim their own conceit,
    I praise my Lord instead.
Their pride falls to destruction,
    Yet I am ever brave,
Assured God's purpose is to judge,
    God's mercy is to save.

Psalm 21

CM (Suggested tunes: St. Anne; Azmon; St. Flavian)

To Your unequalled strength, O Lord,
    Your chosen ones aspire;
Bring to the just sure victory,
    And grant their hearts' desire.

The rulers of the Lord's elect
    Wear crowns of finest gold;
Their lives, once empty, now through faith
    Shall burst with wealth untold.

To those who honor shall bestow
    On God, shall honor come;
And those in whom goodwill abides
    In God will find a home.

In wrath our enemies will fall,
    God's arm puts them to flight;
We gain our blessings by God's grace,
    And vict'ry through God's might.

Psalm 22a

7.6.7.6 D (Suggested tunes: PASSION CHORALE; LLANGLOFFAN)

My God, am I forsaken?
    Why turn from me Your eyes?
Why cease to feel my anguish,
    Or hear my plaintive cries?
The ones who came before me
    Found merit for their trust;
While I, despised, tormented,
    Am cast into the dust.

With scorn my foes deride me,
    Their taunts my faith would move;
Yet firm is my conviction,
    Deep-rooted in Your love.
My God, my sure salvation,
    Be near me all my days;
Whatever may befall me,
    Remain my strength always.

Psalm 22b

CM (Suggested tunes: ELLACOMBE; KINGSFOLD; AZMON)

I come with praise before the Lord,
  Release me from all strife;
The poor will feast at tables full
  And find eternal life.

The far-flung corners of the earth
  Shall turn to God and sing;
And nations of the world shall rise
  To hail the Lord as King.

The mighty on their knees will bow;
  As mortals, they discern
That, as from dust God gave them breath,
  To dust they shall return.

Descendants of the coming years
  Who walk the paths well trod
Will sing to children yet unborn
  The mighty acts of God.

Psalm 23

CMD (Suggested tunes: FOREST GREEN; CRIMOND;
MORNING SONG)

As faithful shepherds tend their flocks,
    So God will care for me;
And from God's store of grace my needs
    Are met abundantly.
In pastures green, by waters still,
    My soul new life does take;
And in the paths of righteousness
    I follow, for God's sake.

When death surrounds I will not fear,
    God's strength dispels my dread;
I hold God's blessing in my heart
    And face my fear instead.
For as a lamb, my comfort rests
    Upon the Shepherd's rod,
To bring me home, where'er I stray
    Into the fold of God.

A bounteous feast for me is placed
    In presence of my foes;
My head with oil the Lord anoints,
    My cup with grace o'erflows.
The loving-kindness of the Lord
    Is mine for all my days;
And in God's house for evermore
    I'll join the songs of praise.

Psalm 24

10.10.10.10 (Suggested tunes: TOULON; ELLERS)

Lord, all creation with Your name resounds,
    And all who dwell within earth's ample bounds;
Ever above the seas have mountains stood,
    Planted by Your design upon the flood.

Who shall to Zion's sacred heights ascend?
    Within God's house, whom shall the Lord defend?
The true, the meek, the righteous and the pure
    Shall in God's courts of blessing long endure.

Lift high your heads, O gates, before the Lord!
    Unfold to greet our God with one accord!
Break free the bonds that bind you to your walls!
    Welcome the mighty God, the Lord of all!

Lift up your heads, O ancient doors, and give
    Passage unbarred to God, in whom we live;
Who is this God, who merits such delight?
    The Lord Almighty, crowned in glory bright!

Psalm 25

CM (Suggested tunes: MORNING SONG; MARTYRDOM; IRISH)

To You, O Lord, I lift my soul,
In You, O God, I trust;
Let vanity be put to shame,
And languish in the dust.

Make me to know Your paths, O God,
And lead me in Your way;
To learn such saving truth my heart
Shall meditate each day.

The Lord is goodness, truth, and love,
God's path the saints have trod;
And children of the covenant
Still walk beside their God.

Be mindful of Your mercy, Lord,
Your love from ages past;
Forgive the weakness of my youth
And bring me home at last.

Psalm 26

LM (Suggested tunes: ROCKINGHAM; GERMANY; BOURBON)

Be now my judge, O Lord, my God,
    For I have walked among the just;
With confidence, I shall not fall,
    For always You have been my trust.

Test me, O Lord, before Your sight;
    The secrets of my heart reveal;
And for the wrongs which mar my cause,
    To Your great mercy, I appeal.

I flee from empty boasts of pride,
    And shun the dismal haunts of woe;
Their evil threats, my path would spurn;
    Your truth, my light, where'er I go.

O God, I love Your holy house,
    Where justice clothed in love resides;
The lure of earth cannot corrupt
    The soul which in Your grace abides.

Psalm 27

8.7.8.7 D (Suggested tunes: ABBOT'S LEIGH; BEACH SPRING;
AUSTRIAN HYMN)

God, my light and my salvation,
    In whose strength my hope is laid;
Confident in my salvation,
    I shall never be afraid.
Evil hosts may rise against me,
    Wars distress, and flesh decays;
Yet the cruelest death imagined
    But begins my song of praise.

Shelter me within the haven
    Of Your house all time to come;
On the rock of Your protection,
    Let me safely find a home.
Lift me high above the legions
    Who would rail against God's word:
O'er the tumult of division
    Make my cry for peace be heard.

When my trust is disappointed,
    Faith confronted with disdain;
Friend and foe defeat my purpose,
    Even then You will sustain.
Had I not with eyes believing
    Seen the goodness of Your face,
Never could I taste such pleasure,
    Nor await such saving grace.

Psalm 28

LM (Suggested tunes: DU MEINER SEELEN; BOURBON; ERHALT UNS, HERR)

O Lord, my strength, to You I cry;
  Ignore my plea, and I shall die.
My soul would perish in the grave,
  Except for Your desire to save.

In awe, I lift my heart to You,
  Whose grace is broad, whose love is true;
From my transgressions, let me be
  Through Your redemption, pure and free.

Thanks be to God, who hears my prayer;
  With me Your joy and favor share;
My strength, my shield, my health always;
  Forever let me sing Your praise!

Psalm 29

8.7.8.7 D (Suggested tunes: AUSTRIAN HYMN;
HYFDRYOL; EBENEZER)

All on earth and all in heaven,
    Raise to God a song on high;
Strength unmeasured, love unbounded,
    God alone we glorify.
At God's voice the clouds assemble,
    Thunder roars and torrents fall;
Earth shall quake before God's presence,
    Mountains tremble at God's call.

Trees shall bow in awe and wonder,
    Bend their branches to the ground;
From God's lips one word in anger
    Wreaks destruction all around.
But the Word which sets in motion
    Such travails can make them cease;
That same voice which tumult beckons
    On a gentler breath speaks peace.

Psalm 30

8.7.8.7 D (Suggested tunes: ABBOT'S LEIGH; HYFRYDOL; BEACH SPRING)

Sing to God, that all may hear you!
    God, whose arms can lift and save;
By Your healing touch, revive us,
    Life restore beyond the grave.
Praise we now our sure salvation,
    God, the holy One above;
End the night so dimmed by anguish
    With the sunrise of Your love.

God, whose wrath we more than merit;
    God, whose grace we cannot earn;
When the pride of human nature
    From Your way tempts us to turn,
Then we cry to You for mercy,
    "Can the tomb repeat God's praise?"
Through Your goodness, yet redeem us,
    Make us faithful all our days.

Change our sorrow to rejoicing,
    Clothe with gladness all despair;
Cause unsteady feet that stumble
    Now to dance beneath Your care.
Dry the tears we shed in mourning,
    Give us steadfast hope always;
Fill our hearts with expectation,
    And our songs with thanks and praise.

Psalm 31a

LM (Suggested tunes: WAREHAM; O WALY WALY;
VENI CREATOR SPIRITUS)

O Lord, in whom my soul confides;
    My refuge sure amid the strife;
O let me not in shame reside,
    But through Your grace reclaim my life.

Always my rock, my sure defense,
    My fortress which no force can break;
Remain my guide, and lead me forth
    To praise You for Your mercy's sake.

My life, my days, are in Your hand,
    Naught can the threat of death remove;
Turn now to me Your shining face,
    And save me through Your steadfast love.

Psalm 31b

9.8.9.8 (Suggested tune: ST. CLEMENT)

Be gracious, Lord, for I, in anguish,
    Your heartfelt mercy now implore;
The very heart within me planted
    Can bear its grief alone no more.

My eyes have wasted all their crying,
    My life with sorrow melts away;
The loving thoughts of those around me
    In scorn and mem'ry fast decay.

Amid the pain of their denial,
    I come, O Lord, to You for grace;
My trust is in Your steadfast mercy,
    I glory in Your smiling face.

Psalm 32

7.6.7.6 D (Suggested tunes: Munich; Es Flog Ein
Kleins Waldvogelein; Valet Will Ich Dir Geben)

How blest those whose transgressions
    The Lord forgives through grace;
Who, as the heirs of mercy,
    Find peace before God's face.
The heart with guilt so heavy
    It bends to bear the strain
Can yield God its affliction
    And claim its strength again.

The Lord with absolution
    Will greet the penitent,
And send the dawn of mercy
    Before the night is spent.
God to the meek and lowly
    A hiding place shall be;
In danger, their salvation;
    From sin, their liberty.

Instill in me Your wisdom,
    Instruct me in Your ways;
Grant but a word of pardon
    And I respond with praise.
God's steadfast love surrounds me,
    And doubts shall soon depart;
Redeemed, my soul rejoices,
    And gladness fills my heart.

Psalm 33

CMD (Suggested tunes: ELLACOMBE;
FOREST GREEN; AZMON)

Rejoice, you righteous, in the Lord,
　In song your voices raise;
Awake the harp and psaltery,
　Lift up God's name in praise!
For by God's word the heavens
　Were hung; the sea, the land,
And all that fill the firmament
　Were made at God's command.

Let ev'ry nation of the earth
　Unite with one accord,
And humbly lay their heartfelt prayers
　In awe before the Lord.
How happy are God's children,
　How blest God's chosen heirs,
For surely an inheritance
　Of glory shall be theirs!

Behold, God's ever-watchful eye
　Sees through our dark despair;
The arms of Grace encircle us
　With strong, yet tender care;
The hope of countless ages,
　Who sets at peace our fears,
God's mercy and compassion
　Shall follow all our years.

Psalm 34

CM (Suggested tunes: ST. MAGNUS; ST. STEPHEN; MCKEE)

Unto the Lord my praise I sing,
   God's goodness ever bless;
The proud convictions of my soul
   Speak of God's righteousness.

Come, magnify the Lord with me!
   Together bring God praise,
Whose presence overcomes all fear,
   And glory lights our days.

O taste and see, the Lord is good!
   How blest are they who place
Reliance on God's steadfast love,
   And trust God's saving grace.

So great the trials of the just,
   Yet greater is God's will,
That from the threat'ning chill of death
   God's truth redeems us still.

Psalm 35

LM (Suggested tunes: DEO GRACIAS;
ROCKINGHAM; WAREHAM)

Defend my cause, O Lord, with them
   Whose might against my life contend;
To their assault, confusion bring;
   To Your elect, salvation send.

Confound and shame all evil ways
   Of those who work iniquity;
Their limbs entangle in the snare
   Which craftily they set for me.

I cannot plead God's wrath on them
   Unless I, too, God's judgment own;
Let my desire for righteousness
   Keep me from standing trial alone.

They shout for joy, who in God's courts
   Will find an everlasting home;
God's justice and prosperity
   Shall ever be my joyful song.

Psalm 36

LM (Suggested tunes: O WALY WALY; MARYTON;
PUER NOBIS NASCITUR)

Your gifts, O Lord, surpass the heav'ns,
  Your faithfulness, the clouds above;
How matchless is Your righteousness;
  How dear is Your redeeming love.

Beneath the shadow of Your wings
  All people banquet at Your board;
They drink the cup of pure delights
  And taste the pleasure of the Lord.

God is the wellspring of my life,
  And in God's light, I light shall see;
The pure of heart true favor find,
  And in God's law their liberty.

Psalm 37

7.6.7.6 D (Suggested tunes: AURELIA; LLANGLOFFAN;
VALET WILL ICH DIR GEBEN)

Fret not the crowds of evil,
　　The fortunes they amass;
Like blossoms they shall wither,
　　And fade as new-mown grass.
But trust the Lord, whose goodness
　　Your faithfulness inspires;
Delight in God, whose graciousness
　　Fulfills your heart's desires.

Commit your ways unto the Lord,
　　Who vindication brings;
The soul that patiently attends
　　A song of vict'ry sings.
God's foes shall fall in anguish,
　　The meek possess the land;
While they as by the sword are drawn,
　　We feast from God's own hand.

Though hosts may deal affliction,
　　The Lord our strength shall be;
God's might shall burst the nets they cast
　　And set the captives free.
Salvation is the promise
　　The Lord preserves in store
For those who live in goodness
　　And trust God evermore.

Psalm 38

LM (Suggested tunes: ERHALT UNS, HERR;
KEDRON; BOURBON)

O Lord, I pray, judge not my cause
    In wrath, though I transgress Your laws;
The burden of my guilt would take
    My life, but for Your mercy's sake.

I ache in spirit, heart, and mind,
    For peace in God alone I find;
My tongue too long refused to share
    The pain my sins have brought to bear.

The anguish of unrighteousness
    To Your good grace I now confess;
The tears I shed for selfish gain
    Are powerless to cleanse the stain.

To You, O God, in hope I pray
    That You, who ever shows the way,
Will patience and devotion send
    That I may follow to the end.

Psalm 39

CM (Suggested tunes: DETROIT; CRIMOND; LAND OF REST)

My words a wicked tongue subdued,
  They passed without a sound;
In silence I withheld the grief
  Which compassed me around.

How long, O Lord, before my end?
  How many are the days
Until my frail and feeble soul
  Shall see Your courts of praise?

The things of earth are vanity;
  They pass before the night;
False treasures cast a tempting gleam,
  Then fade before our sight.

My hope, my confidence, my faith,
  O God, I rest at night;
A stranger, grant me strength to dwell
  Forever in Your light.

Psalm 40

7.6.8.6.8.6.8.6 (Suggested tune: St. Christopher)

With patient hope I waited for God to hear my plea;
    And from the depths of my despair, God's arm
    uplifted me.
My feet are set upon the rock, where none can make
me fall;
    My mouth is filled with songs of praise to God, my
    all in all.

How blest the truly faithful, who trust the Lord of hosts;
    They set no store in empty pride, no hope in
    idle boasts.
The treasures of our fragile minds, false gods of wealth
and fame,
    Are naught to those who know God's works, and kneel
    before God's name.

The ancient cost of pardon God's law no more requires;
    A willing and compliant heart fulfills the Lord's desire.
I always sing of God's goodwill, God's praise is
my delight;
    My joy, to know this humble life is pleasing in
    God's sight.

I celebrate the goodness that God has shown to me:
    The patience to endure my cross, the grace to set
    me free.
The gifts I truly prize are such that earth cannot remove:
    God's favor for my faithfulness, and mercy for
    my love.

Psalm 41

LM (Suggested tunes: Germany; Du Meiner Seelen; Hamburg)

O blest are they who in their love
    Compassion hold for those in need;
For they shall find, when faced by foes,
    The Lord is their defense indeed.

When all the evils earth can dream
    Are cast on me, my faith to break;
Their rage I temper through God's grace,
    And bear them boldly for God's sake.

The hands which shared my broken bread,
    My love with their deceit repaid;
And friends whose trust I counted mine
    Have left me wounded and betrayed.

To me, O Lord, in mercy turn;
    Your favor, my most treasured prize;
My mouth shall sing redemption's song,
    And tears of love wash clean my eyes.

BOOK II

Psalm 42

9.8.9.8 (Suggested tune: ST. CLEMENT)

Cool streams a breathless deer desires.
    So longs my soul for You, my Lord;
I thirst to see Your face, O God,
    My heart, Your dwelling place adored.

"Where is your God?" they ask of me,
    When tears have been my only food;
How long, O Lord, till doubts dispel
    My tattered mem'ries of Your good?

Deep calls to deep, and oceans roar,
    Their thunder my destruction brings;
Yet steadfast love my hope sustains,
    My tongue divine assurance sings.

Why grieves my soul and stirs my heart
    When shallow threats of death assail?
My hope, my rock, my sure defense
    Remains the God of Israel.

Psalm 43

CMD (Suggested tunes: KINGSFOLD; FOREST GREEN; RESIGNATION)

Pronounce for me Your judgment, God,
    Defend my righteous part
Against the vain, ungodly foes
    Who would corrupt my heart.
For You, O God, have been my strength
    In generations past;
Though I may doubt, Your presence will
    Protect me to the last.

Send out Your light and shining truth
    To lead the faithful home;
May I within Your holy hill
    Delight for years to come.
And in Your courts of joy and peace
    I will to You always
Repay the goodness poured on me
    With songs of thanks and praise.

Psalm 44

CMD (Suggested tunes: KINGSFOLD; ELLACOMBE; MATERNA)

Your goodness, Lord, and wondrous deeds
    Across the years are told
To generations yet unborn
    By faithful hearts of old.
By Your own hand the nations fell,
    New lands did come to be;
Through Your own might were foes subdued,
    And by Your Word set free.

I cannot trust in sword and shield,
    Except the Lord will guide;
Nor can I claim the victory,
    But You are at my side.
O help me, God, not to forget
    Your goodness shown to me;
Lest in the hour I need You most,
    I, too, forgotten be.

God knows the secrets of my heart,
    The weakness of my will;
I cry, "Awake!" God does not sleep,
    Yet deigns to love me still.
God, build my hope and confidence
    That none can dare remove;
Make me as steadfast in my faith
    As You are in Your love.

Psalm 45a

7.7.7.7 (Suggested tunes: MONKLAND; SONG 13)

How our hearts with joy abound,
    With Your beauty all around;
Words are feeble to express
    Your great love and righteousness.

Fairer still than human frame,
    Ever to our eyes the same;
Steadfast love shines from Your face;
    From Your lips flow words of grace.

Yours the scepter, Yours the throne;
    You to us are God alone;
Vast the mercies to us giv'n:
    Wealth of earth, and joy of heav'n.

Psalm 45b

7.7.7.7.7.7 (Suggested tunes: REDHEAD 76; DIX; RATISBON)

Sons and daughters of the earth,
  Set your minds beyond your kin;
Great the Lord, and great the courts
  God's elect may enter in.
Glorious gifts, for mercy's sake,
  We are chosen to partake.

Come with joy and highest praise
  Into God's most sacred hall;
Let your song of praise proclaim:
  God alone is Lord of all.
Generations yet to come
  Find in You a loving home.

Psalm 46

8.7.8.7.8.7 (Suggested tunes: WESTMINSTER ABBEY;
LAUDA ANIMA; PICARDY)

God, our strength and mighty fortress,
    God, our refuge in distress;
God, whose promise is deliv'rance,
    God, whose law is righteousness;
Though the earth with fear may tremble,
    None can shake Your faithfulness.

In the city of the Holy,
    Rivers flow and streams run pure;
Where the Lord abides in splendor,
    There God's people dwell secure.
In their hearts, God's love will flourish,
    Through their faith, God's Word endure.

Come, behold God's matchless wonders,
    See the bounty of God's hand;
Gifts beyond our expectations,
    Works too great to understand.
Sound God's might in songs of glory
    Sung to earth's most distant land.

Psalm 47

8.7.8.7.8.7.7 (Suggested tune: CWM RHONDDA)

Clap your hands, O faithful people!
   Shout to God a song of praise!
From the dust of conquered nations,
   God a realm of grace shall raise.
In appointed courts of glory,
   Faithful to God's name always,
May we prosper all our days.

With a shout, and blast of trumpet,
   God shall mount a throne on high;
Let our praise, as finest incense,
   Rise to meet God in the sky.
Fill the world with glad rejoicing,
   Heav'n shall sing, and earth reply,
All God's works to glorify.

Let your hearts be filled with gladness,
   As the Lord your life shall bless;
Live as heirs of God's great justice,
   Wear the cloak of righteousness.
God will grant us earth's dominion,
   All things good, and nothing less,
For our gift of faithfulness.

Psalm 48

10.10.11.11 (Suggested tunes: LYONS; HANOVER;
LAUDATE DOMINUM)

How great is the Lord and worthy of praise,
    Whose glory above Mount Zion displays!
In light of God's splendor our cities are dust;
    Eternal our refuge, unquestioned our trust.

The rulers of earth are shaken with fright,
    When God, filled with wrath, appears in their sight;
But we as the chosen have witnessed God's heart,
    And at its remembrance, all fears soon depart.

The far-fashioned bounds of earth lift their voice,
    And for God's goodwill, the mountains rejoice;
Whose righteousness follows the course of our days;
    Whatever our pathway, our Guide for always.

Psalm 49

7.6.7.6 D (Suggested tunes: AURELIA; MUNICH; LLANGLOFFAN)

Hear this, all folk together,
   Of low and high degree;
Both rich and poor, speak wisdom,
   And ponder faithfully
How God alone the ransom
   For mortal life can pay,
How mortal wealth, like shadows,
   Fades with the dying day.

All life in time must perish,
   The grave becomes its bed;
False pride and vain ambition
   Decay among the dead.
How foolish they whose fortunes
   In earthly molds are cast;
While human love dies with them,
   The love of God will last.

The glimmer of our treasure
   Will not salvation win,
For God shall judge our glory
   By light that shines within.
The joy we hold sufficient
   Is slight before God's eyes,
For naught on earth can capture
   The taste of Paradise.

Psalm 50

CMD (Suggested tunes: ELLACOMBE; FOREST GREEN; KINGSFOLD)

The Mighty One, the Lord of Hosts,
　　Speaks and the world obeys;
From dawn until the setting sun,
　　God's wonder earth displays.
The perfect beauty all around
　　From Zion's height shines forth;
And stars across the firmament
　　So brightly beam their worth.

God comes, not with a silent form,
　　But riding on the winds;
Before God's face, the raging storm
　　Its blasts of thunder sends.
All hail the Judge, in bold array,
　　Who weighs our righteousness
Against all sin, and with whose grace
　　Deigns faithful hearts to bless.

The heav'ns declare Your justice, Lord,
　　As endless as the sky;
Against the taunts of disbelief,
　　Our God will testify.
Receive my heartfelt gift of thanks
　　As honor to Your might;
Refresh my faith with each new day;
　　Protect me through the night.

Psalm 51

CM (Suggested tunes: LAND OF REST;
ST. FLAVIAN; DUNDEE)

Have mercy, Lord, according to
    The measure of Your love;
Blot out my sin, and from my heart
    All wickedness remove.

The failings of my deeds and thoughts
    Are ever in my sight;
Release me from the path of death,
    And set my course aright.

Into my secret heart send truth,
    Let wisdom in me grow;
O wash the evil from my hands,
    And make me pure as snow.

A clean and upright heart, O Lord,
    Exchange for mine of stone;
Your Holy Spirit meld with mine,
    And leave me not alone.

A contrite heart is Your desire,
    My offering, the same;
My lips unlatch, my mouth engage
    Your praises to proclaim.

Psalm 52

8.7.8.7 D (Suggested tunes: EBENEZER; HOLY MANNA)

Why your boast, O wicked mortals?
　　Why your pride in vain deceit?
All your efforts work their malice,
　　God's true causes to defeat.
Like a sword, your evil cunning
　　Cuts the righteous to the core;
But the Lord rejects deception,
　　And endures your hate no more.

Then the righteous shall with laughter
　　Celebrate your earned demise;
Raise new virtue from your ashes,
　　Speak the truth above your lies.
By God's justice shall the faithful
　　Claim your loss as their own gain;
Evermore God's praises render,
　　Ever in God's house remain.

Psalm 53

7.7.7.7 D (Suggested tunes: Aberystwyth; Nun Komm, Der Heiden Heiland)

How the foolish in their hearts
    Can the law of God deny!
All their evil deeds are vain,
    Every oath a vicious lie.
God from heav'n the earth surveys,
    All must pass before God's eyes;
Is there one the Lord calls good?
    Is there none God counts as wise?

All have turned in their conceit
    To their own innate desires;
Faith has fled the doubt of scorn,
    Selfish love with hate conspires.
But the dreadful day shall come,
    Retribution for their wrongs;
Then shall all our cries of grief
    Be transformed to joyful songs.

Psalm 54

CM (Suggested tunes: MARTYRDOM; LAND OF REST; IRISH)

O save me, God, and hear my cry;
    My prayer to You ascends;
And vindicate me by Your might;
    On You my hope depends.

You, Lord, my help shall ever be,
    Though evil pow'rs assail;
From their designs, my life redeem
    Through grace which cannot fail.

My sacrifice I offer You,
    As thanks for all Your grace;
Let me so live, that I in death
    May greet You face to face.

Psalm 55

LM (Suggested tunes: ERHALT UNS, HERR; ROCKINGHAM;
DU MEINER SEELEN)

Give ear, O Lord, unto my prayer;
    Hide not Yourself from my distress.
The sound of hatred fills the air,
    The fears of death upon me press.

O that my wings were like a dove,
    I'd fly away and be at rest,
Far from the raging war remove
    To prosper in the wilderness.

My foes I counted once as friends
    Now break the heart that held them dear;
They work deceit to gain their ends,
    And fellowship confound with fear.

I cast my burden on the Lord,
    And through my life God will sustain;
The righteous praise with one accord,
    And in God's endless love remain.

Psalm 56

CM (Suggested tunes: ST. STEPHEN; CAITHNESS; CRIMOND)

Be gracious unto me, O Lord,
　　For great is my distress;
At ev'ry hand, my foes conspire
　　An end to righteousness.

When bound by fear of their assault,
　　My faith in You I rest;
If You I trust with spirit sure,
　　With vict'ry am I blessed.

You, Lord, have seen what I endure,
　　Each step along the way;
O keep a record of my tears
　　And turn each threat away.

My faithful vows I must perform
　　For God, whose Word I praise;
That God to me might faithful be
　　Throughout my future days.

Psalm 57

7.6.7.6 D (Suggested tune: LLANGLOFFAN)

Be merciful to me, O God,
　　In You alone I trust,
That in the shadow of Your wings
　　I rise above the dust.
Send forth Your sure salvation
　　To me before I fall,
And for Your favor I shall claim
　　You as the Lord of all.

My heart is steadfast in its faith
　　That You will hear my voice;
With confidence, my soul, awake,
　　And in Your truth rejoice!
Such love to me surpasses
　　My talents to proclaim;
Yet with my life I celebrate
　　The glories of Your name.

Psalm 58

8.7.8.7 D (Suggested tunes: EBENEZER; HOLY MANNA;
PLEADING SAVIOR)

Those who judge the deeds of others
　　Must be led by righteousness;
Lest the verdict of injustice
　　Their own evil works express.
Can the guilty find them guilty,
　　Who by grace should pardon see?
Can they bind the poor in shackles
　　Who by right should be set free?

From their birth the hosts of evil
　　At the just in anger rave;
Their assaults will sting but vanish,
　　Justice reigns beyond the grave.
Though like thorns their threats may pierce us,
　　They those same thorns shall embrace;
God, who shall decree their sentence,
　　Rescues us through boundless grace.

Psalm 59

LM (Suggested tunes: WHEN JESUS WEPT; KEDRON;
ROCKINGHAM)

Deliver me from all my foes,
   Subdue the hands my blood would shed;
Let rampant pride with grace be bound,
   And starving hate with love be fed.

O Lord of hosts, I You implore,
   Rise to my aid, and You shall view
The mockery and bitter scorn
   I through my faith endure for You.

My God, my fortress and my strength,
   All foul profanity remove;
Let lies with truth be overcome,
   And empty threats with words of love.

My song, O Lord, shall ever be
   Of faith and justice all my days;
Since You the vict'ry has assured,
   Who else stands worthy of my praise?

Psalm 60

LM (Suggested tunes: KEDRON; BOURBON; PROSPECT)

The Lord in wrath, and rightly so,
    Should us abandon to our sin;
Yet, grace such anger can subdue,
    And bring us to God's fold again.

The earth may shake, the mountains fall,
    The desert plain apart be rent;
No vict'ry comes but by God's hand;
    No peace without the Lord's consent.

What help have we without God's aid
    To strengthen us against the sword?
Our faith is in God's promise laid,
    Our hope is anchored in God's Word.

Psalm 61

8.7.8.7 (Suggested tunes: STUTTGART; CHARLESTOWN; RATHBUN)

Hear my cry, O Rock of Ages,
    To my earnest prayer, give ear;
Grant me refuge from disaster,
    Confidence to vanquish fear.

You, O God, have heard my bidding,
    Once delivered, yet the same;
You will ne'er forget the promise
    Giv'n to all who fear Your name.

In Your tent afford protection,
    Shelter me beneath Your wing;
Let my tongue, filled with Your praises,
    In Your courts forever sing.

Psalm 62

LM (Suggested tunes: WAREHAM; MARYTON; ROCKINGHAM)

My soul, O God, in silence waits;
　My hope secure without a sound;
The Lord's my refuge and my rock,
　In whom the joys of life abound.

I set my trust in You beyond
　The futile boasts of mortal pride;
With confidence I hold Your prize,
　And cast dishonest claims aside.

Into my silence, You have said
　That goodness rests with You above;
The recompense for my delight:
　A share of Your unfailing love.

Psalm 63

CM (Suggested tunes: Caithness; Ptomey; St. Agnes)

O God, my God, with eagerness
    I long to see Your face;
Lost in a dry and barren land,
    I thirst to taste Your grace.

Your endless mercies, Lord, are mine
    As Your appointed heir;
Your steadfast love throughout my life
    Is joy beyond compare.

My soul has feasted at Your board,
    Your glories fill my sight;
I spend my waking hours in praise,
    And pray my thoughts at night.

Throughout my life You are my help,
    My soul is bold to sing;
And after death, I'll rest beneath
    The shadow of Your wing.

Psalm 64

CM (Suggested tunes: PTOMEY; ST. STEPHEN; MORNING SONG)

Before the savage threat of foes,
    My earnest prayers attend;
From their most sinister intent,
    O Lord, Your child defend.

Their tongues, like swords, assail my faith,
    With bitter words of woe;
My path is set with cunning snares
    No matter where I go.

Lord, You alone their vengeance turn,
    And justice will impart;
In righteousness, I shall rejoice,
    And hold You in my heart.

Psalm 65

11.11.11.11 (Suggested tunes: ST. DENIO; FOUNDATION)

The praises of Zion, O God, are Your due;
  Your mercies are countless, our merits are few;
The weight of transgressions Your grace will remove,
  And give life we cherish, redeemed by Your love.

Your strength has established the sea and the plain;
  Each day all creation Your praise sings again;
The God of salvation, our hope for always,
  A shelter in darkness, the light of our days.

The earth's endless bounty, Lord, let us preserve;
  Its richness and splendor we less than deserve;
The cycle of seasons gives sense to the year,
  An autumn for harvest, a springtime of cheer!

Psalm 66a

7.7.7.7.7.7 (Suggested tune: DIX)

Make a joyful noise to God!
　　All creation sings Your praise!
Great Your wonders here displayed,
　　Unexcelled throughout our days.
Glorious is Your sacred name,
　　Ages old, yet still the same.

Come and see what God has done;
　　Great the blessings to the just;
Walked the chosen through the sea;
　　Brought their enemies to dust.
Let us lift a thankful voice
　　For God's mercies, and rejoice!

Bless the Lord, our refuge sure;
　　Let your song of praise be heard!
By whose justice, we are tried;
　　By whose grace, our guilt deferred.
When our life's sure end shall come,
　　Bring us to Your heav'nly home.

Psalm 66b

CM (Suggested tunes: ST. PETER; MCKEE; ST. ANNE)

O bless the Lord now, one and all,
    Let songs of praise resound!
For in the midst of our distress,
    God's presence can be found.

The ancient law required of me
    Burnt off'rings for my part;
But as a nobler sacrifice,
    I offer God my heart.

Would that the world in ev'ry place
    Knew God as I have known;
God shares my joy, and in my grief
    Will leave me not alone.

Bless God, all you who would the lies
    Of sinful lips disprove;
With truth God shall sustain your way,
    Your life with steadfast love.

Psalm 67

8.7.8.7 D (Suggested tunes: HYFRYDOL; AUSTRIAN HYMN, HYMN TO JOY)

God of mercy and compassion,
    Lord of love, redeeming grace;
Let the brightness of Your glory
    Shine upon us in this place.
Show all nations Your salvation,
    End our dark, long-suff'ring days;
Cause our hearts with joy to greet You;
    Fill the earth with songs of praise!

Sing with joy, the Lord is coming!
    God with us, Immanuel,
Brings in triumph our salvation,
    Death shall die, and life prevail.
In the wisdom of God's justice
    Righteousness shall conquer scorn;
On God's head, the crown of nations;
    In God's heart, a crown of thorns.

Come, Almighty, now and bless us,
    Your great covenant renew;
May creation yield its increase,
    Find its greatest gift in You.
Ev'ry tongue shall call You blessed,
    Ev'ry voice a welcome bring
To the Word of God incarnate;
    Earth shall bow, and heaven sing!

Psalm 68

6.6.11.6.6.11 D (Suggested tune: ASH GROVE)

Arise, Lord, and hasten,
　　All woe, swiftly chasten,
As smoke in the whirlwind
　　So drive it away!
While malice shall perish,
　　Your goodness we cherish,
With joy shall the righteous
　　All sadness betray!

Sing praise to God only,
　　We poor folk, and lonely,
For out of compassion
　　God cares for us all.
The blessings we savor
　　Are ours by God's favor;
Whose goodness, like raindrops,
　　On deserts shall fall.

All realms of creation
　　Now sing with elation
Their praise to the Maker
　　Of earth and of sea.
The heav'ns, in their glory,
　　Resound with the story
Of God's matchless power
　　All ages to be.

Ascribe to God wonder,
　　Whose voice, like the thunder,
Can shatter the stillness
　　And call us to praise;
Whose Spirit life gave us,
　　Whose mercy can save us,
The Source of our being,
　　The Joy of our days!

Psalm 69

9.8.9.8.8.8 (Suggested tunes: WER NUR DEN LIEBEN GOTT;
O DASS ICH TAUSEND ZUNGEN HATTE)

Save me, O God, lest I should perish;
    None else can raise me from the mire;
My only hope for sure salvation
    Is that my life is Your desire.
My throat is parched as desert sod,
    And dimming eyes await my God.

Countless are those who hate me sorely;
    Mighty are they who would destroy!
Let bitter scorn not spoil my honor,
    Nor vain contention steal my joy.
Since for my faith, I suffer shame,
    Save me, O Lord, I trust Your name.

My hope, Your promise to redeem me,
    Shall be a shield against despair;
Who can assail me with a vengeance,
    If at my side, You, Lord, are there?
Make evil fail in its deceit,
    Swallow its pride in self-defeat.

O could I sing Your praise forever,
    Offer my thanks to You aright;
More than a sacrifice of riches,
    A grateful heart is Your delight!
Let earth and heav'n, as with one voice,
    Sound forth Your glory, and rejoice!

Psalm 70

8.7.8.7 (Suggested tunes: STUTTGART; CHARLESTOWN)

May the Lord be pleased to save me;
    Hasten, for the time draws near,
When the vicious hosts of evil
    At my shattered camp appear.

Turn them back, the proud, the mighty,
    Let them fall in their conceit;
Bid the foes that would o'erwhelm me
    Trace their path in swift retreat.

I alone cannot withstand them,
    God, my strength, be at my side;
In Your courts, secure, protected,
    Soon, O Lord, let me abide.

Psalm 71

CM (Suggested tunes: AZMON; ST. PETER; ST. FLAVIAN)

In You, O Lord, I put my trust;
    Preserve from fear and shame
The righteous servant in distress
    Who calls upon Your name.

For from the moment of my birth
    Through my allotted days,
I shall not waver in my trust,
    Or cease to sing Your praise.

O God, be never far from me,
    Your favor I implore;
I'll hope in You all time to come,
    And praise You evermore.

Psalm 72

8.7.8.7.6.6.6.6.7 (Suggested tune: EIN' FESTE BURG)

Grant justice, Lord, to those who rule;
    Let righteousness compel their hand;
Their courts shall bear prosperity,
    And serve the poor throughout the land.
O Lord, our cause defend;
Deliv'rance quickly send
    To those who, bound in chains
    Of greed and selfish gains,
Submit themselves to Your command.

As long as sun and stars of space
    Walk their divine-appointed round;
Long as endures our feeble race,
    The blessings of the Lord abound.
Like rains that feed the field,
    Our Lord to us will yield
    The bounty and the peace
Which God will never cease
    To shower where true faith is found.

God's righteousness extends to all
    Who seek assurance in distress;
The weak who in their anguish bend
    When hate and violence oppress.
As golden sheaves of grain,
    God's harvest we remain;
    All praise to God above!
Who crowns our life with love,
    O bless God's name forever.

BOOK III

Psalm 73

SMD (Suggested tunes: TERRA BEATA;
ICH TREULICH STILL)

The Lord is surely good
   To those whose hearts are pure;
To those upright, who in God's sight
   Are just, the path is sure.
But all along my way,
   The tempter's charms assail;
Lord, cast aside ambitious pride,
   My faith in You prevail.

The proud with self are clothed,
   And greed their will commands;
Vain hearts are rent with discontent
   That God their praise demands.
As slaves they hold us fast,
   And all goodwill oppress;
They use deceit for our defeat,
   And wrong for righteousness.

I know my weakness, Lord,
   The ease with which I fall;
At Your right hand, I long to stand
   And claim You Lord of all!
What hope have I in earth,
   Or glory yet to claim?
My flesh is frail, my heart may fail,
   But love still speaks Your name.

Psalm 74

7.7.7.7 D (Suggested tunes: ABERYSTWYTH; NUN KOMM;
DER HEIDEN HEILAND)

Lord, why do You cast us off?
    Why dismiss us to the dead?
Why consume with fiery rage
    Pastures where Your sheep once fed?
When Your temple, like Your Law,
    Is by hateful hands destroyed,
Can we not but mourn the loss
    Of Your peace we once enjoyed?

Filled with wonder, we recall
    Mercies far beyond our dreams;
Seas did part to yield a path;
    Arid fields were fed with streams.
Life You gave where life was lost,
    Gardens in the wilderness;
Have we so refused to love,
    That You, too, refuse to bless?

Know our grief, and help us, Lord,
    To regain our favored place;
Bring us home into Your fold;
    Reinstate us in Your grace.
Your great promise to redeem
    Made to us, may we proclaim;
Make those worthy of Your love
    Who in faith Your love proclaim.

Psalm 75

6.7.6.7.6.6.6.6 (Suggested tunes: NUN DANKET ALLE GOTT;
WAS FRAG' ICH; O GOTT, DU FROMMER GOTT)

We give You thanks, O God,
    For such great goodness shown us;
By whose design creates,
    And by whose Name does own us.
To judge with equity,
    God shall appoint a term;
Though earth's dominions shake,
    Its pillars shall stand firm.

The proud will boast no more,
    Nor lift their horns in splendor;
When hosts of God's elect
    Will vanquish the pretender.
All arrogance will fall,
    And in its place is love;
For who in earth compares
    With God, who reigns above?

God's justice, swift and sure,
    To all is equal measure;
The mighty and the meek
    Must answer God's displeasure.
Each one must from the cup
    Of judgment taste their strife:
The wicked, bitter gall;
    The good, eternal life.

Psalm 76

SMD (Suggested tunes: TERRA BEATA; ICH TREULICH STILL)

Throughout the earth, O Lord,
   Is Your dominion spread;
Jerusalem Your temple holds,
   And Zion crowns Your head.
Great thunderbolts of wrath
   Defeat the noise of war;
And true peace reigns when selfish gains
   Entice our greed no more.

Our Lord is to be feared
   By those who would deny
God's matchless splendor and discharge
   The law with but a sigh.
God shall dismiss the proud
   To fret in jealous pride,
And while they yearn, the meek shall learn
   The Lord stands at their side.

Psalm 77

7.7.7.7.7.7 (Suggested tunes: REDHEAD 76; DIX; RATISBON)

Unto You, I cried aloud,
    That my prayer should reach Your ear;
None but God can lift the cloud,
    None to my despair brings cheer.
In the midst of darkest night,
    Set my fearful doubts to flight.

In distress, I will recall
    How the Lord my life has blessed;
How the heroes of my race
    Fought for truth and righteousness;
Liberty is their reward,
    By the strong arm of the Lord.

In the tempest, You are there,
    Calling forth the flood and fire;
Thunder blasts at Your command,
    If its roar meets Your desire.
For a path, the sea did part,
    From Your throne into my heart.

Psalm 78

8.6.8.6.8.6 (Suggested tune: MORNING SONG)

"Give ear, my people, to my Law,"
    Thus did the Lord command;
"My words, though cast in parable,
    Your hearts can understand.
To tell your children of my might
    Is all that I demand!"

Each passing generation sings
    The wonders of the Lord,
That those who follow in their steps
    May be of one accord
To keep God's Law above all else,
    And hold God yet adored.

How marvelous the Lord preserved
    Our kindred in distress;
The sea a path did yield, and springs
    Did feed the wilderness.
No less are we today the heirs
    Of truth and righteousness.

Psalm 79

6.6.8.4 D (Suggested tune: LEONI)

O Lord, the godless boast
   Our legacy is theirs;
Your holy temple lies in ruin,
   Our faith despairs.
Our flesh is torn for meat,
   And blood, like water, shed;
Our bodies wither in the dust,
   Our hope is dead.

How long, O God, how long,
   Your fury, like a fire
Shall blaze until but ash remains
   Of vain desire?
Remember not our sins,
   But mercy to us show;
Let Your compassion meet our need,
   And grace bestow.

Psalm 80

CMD (Suggested tunes: FOREST GREEN; KINGSFOLD)

O Shepherd, hear and lead Your flock,
    As lambs, we crave Your care;
What strength on earth approaches Yours,
    What mercies can compare?
Restore to us a saving faith,
    The radiance of Your face
To lighten and reveal the gift
    Of Your redeeming grace.

Our selfish prayers deserve Your wrath,
    Our pride, a sudden burst;
We have but stones to serve as bread,
    And tears to quell our thirst.
Restore to us a saving faith,
    The radiance of Your face
To lighten and reveal the gift
    Of Your redeeming grace.

Your lineage, like a vine, once spread
    And flourished in the land;
But now the vineyard fails, the fruit
    Lies withered in the sand.
Restore to us a saving faith,
    The radiance of Your face
To lighten and reveal the gift
    Of Your redeeming grace.

Psalm 81

6.6.8.4 D (Suggested tune: LEONI)

O sing to God, our strength;
    In Jacob's God, rejoice!
Let trumpets sound, and with a song
    Lift up your voice!
"I am the Lord your God,"
    Our Maker did declare;
"The same who saves from captive bonds
    And dark despair."

May we unto God's voice
    Be never deaf to heed,
Or mute to sing the praise of God,
    Our Lord indeed!
"For I shall give the best
    The harvest will afford
Unto the faithful and the just,"
    Thus says the Lord!

Psalm 82

7.6.7.6 D (Suggested tune: LLANGLOFFAN)

Within the congregation
   God with the just shall stand;
The pillars of unrighteousness
   Will shake at God's command.
Injustice meets compassion,
   Contempt discovers grace;
And ev'ry source of our delight
   Is banished from this place.

The wicked shall become as blind,
   And struggle on their way;
To them, as darkest, fearful night
   Appears the brightest day.
They fall, but as they stumble,
   The righteous children dance;
They pass in vain; new life we claim
   For our inheritance.

Psalm 83

8.8.8.8.8.8 (Suggested tunes: DAS NEUGEBORNE KINDELEIN; MELITA; VATER UNSER)

In silence, Lord, do not remain;
   Nor hold Your peace beyond my view.
Be still no more; I cannot gain
   The strength I lack, except from You.
My foes conspire with one accord
   To work their hate against the Lord.

The nations rise against the land
   A birthright given by Your Word;
And legions meet on ev'ry hand;
   Your heirs are crushed beneath the sword.
Only by faith in You professed
   Can we rejoice, secure and blessed.

Disperse their arms as worthless dust;
   Cast them, like chaff, before the wind.
Fill them with shame before the just,
   Bare their deceit, Your judgment send.
To shame their pride, make them recall
   That You alone are Lord of all.

Psalm 84

CM (Suggested tunes: LAND OF REST; CAITHNESS; IRISH)

How lovely is Your dwelling place,
　　O Lord of hosts, to me;
Within the grandeur of Your courts
　　My soul desires to be.

The sparrow finds a safe retreat,
　　Secure she takes her rest;
And in Your shelter, for her young
　　The swallow builds her nest.

How blessed are they who in Your house
　　Live out their faithful days;
Their hearts with springs of joy are filled,
　　Their lips with songs of praise!

To make my home with You, O Lord,
　　My hopeful heart aspires;
For there one day outshines the years
　　Spent for my own desires.

O Lord, You are both sun and shield,
　　My sure defense shall be;
How great the happiness is theirs
　　Who trust, and are set free!

Psalm 85

CMD (Suggested tunes: FOREST GREEN; ELLACOMBE; KINGSFOLD)

The Lord has long with favor looked
    Upon the chosen land;
To Jacob's heirs, the wealth of earth
    Is lavished in their hand.
The captive chains of servitude
    Are loosed, the slaves are free;
And through God's grace, the bonds of sin
    Give way to liberty.

Restore to us salvation, Lord,
    Let Your displeasure cease;
And still the tempest of Your wrath
    With gentle winds of peace.
My humble heart the still small voice
    Of Your love yet attends;
The faithful God from death redeems;
    The fearful, God defends.

Your steadfast love and faithfulness
    Will meet us face to face;
The arm of justice, mercy sways;
    The righteous, truth embrace.
May wisdom dwell in human law,
    And justice, courts display;
Let righteousness precede Your steps,
    And guide us on our way.

Psalm 86

LM (Suggested tunes: WAREHAM; ROCKINGHAM; PROSPECT)

Incline Your ear, O Lord, to me,
    For I am poor, and need Your care;
My God, the anchor of my trust;
    The truest answer to my prayer.

You, Lord, have shown to me Your grace,
    In ways beyond my mortal sight;
Before Your face, I lift my soul;
    To sing Your praise is my delight!

With steadfast love and mercy sure,
    God hears confession and forgives;
Redeemed the soul in which God dwells,
    And blessed the heart in which God lives!

All nations shall proclaim You Lord,
    And at Your name all knees shall bend
To glorify Your righteousness
    And sing Your praises without end.

Psalm 87

CM (Suggested tunes: Azmon; St. Anne; St. Flavian)

The city of our God is built
  Upon the holy hill;
Its gates, through ages unexcelled;
  And courts, unchallenged still.

How great the wonders of its past;
  What glories lie in store?
For out of Zion shall the Lord
  Come to us evermore.

All you who sound the harp and pipe,
  Who songs of hope employ,
The day shall come for you to dance,
  When Zion springs with joy!

Psalm 88

7.6.7.6 D (Suggested tunes: LLANGLOFFAN; MUNICH)

O let my prayer approach You,
Attend my mournful plight;
I call for help in daylight,
And cry out in the night.
My soul is full of sorrow,
As one condemned to die;
Once loved, but now forsaken;
My song now but a sigh.

Your anger rests upon me,
Dark shadows hide my ways;
Can broken arms embrace You,
Can death rise up to praise?
Does Your declared affection
Extend beyond the grave?
If I forget to ask You,
Will You forget to save?

But I have not forgotten
My weakness and Your might;
In humble faith, I beg You
To put my fears to flight.
Though all on earth forsake me,
My lover and my friend,
I hold You to Your promise:
Be with me to the end.

Psalm 89a

8.7.8.7 D (Suggested tunes: ABBOT'S LEIGH;
AUSTRIAN HYMN; HYMN TO JOY)

We will ever sing Your mercy,
    Tell abroad Your faithfulness;
Who throughout all generations
    Keeps the covenant to bless.
Sun and stars shall praise Your wonders,
    All the earth, such glories share;
None in heav'n can match Your greatness;
    None below with You compare.

By Your hand is justice measured;
    Judgment rests with you alone;
Truth and mercy go before You,
    Righteousness becomes Your throne.
Blessed are they who own Your wisdom,
    Those who live within Your grace;
In Your favor, hold us near You;
    Make our hearts Your dwelling place.

God who swore great things to Judah,
    Her defense and strength and stay,
Makes with equal faith the promise
    To abide with us today.
Loving-kindness shall embrace us,
    Truth attend us all our days;
If we give to God all honor,
    We shall live to sing God's praise!

Psalm 89b

CM (Suggested tunes: IRISH; ST. ANNE; MCKEE)

The chosen of the Lord shall own
    God's blessing full and free,
Uplifted by the arms of faith
    For all the world to see.

The steadfast truth and love of God
    Outweighs the crush of hate;
The Lord bestows on faithful hearts
    True joys to celebrate.

The holy court which God ordained
    Brings justice swift and sure;
To those who live beneath the law,
    God's mercies will endure.

God's covenant forever stands
    As truth for all to claim,
And generations yet to come
    Will sing God's holy name.

BOOK IV

Psalm 90

LM (Suggested tunes: DUKE STREET; TRURO;
PUER NOBIS NASCITUR)

Lord, You have been our dwelling place
    From past to coming age the same;
The mountains rise to greet Your face,
    The earth proclaims her Maker's name.

Each generation fades as grass,
    And flesh as dust returns to sod;
A thousand years spent here below
    Are but as yesterday to God.

Teach us to measure all our days,
    That wisdom may our purpose guide;
Each moment fill with righteousness,
    And keep us ever at Your side.

Our mornings may You fill with love,
    And grant us grace when day is past;
That all our life may favor find,
    Till we shall be with You at last.

Psalm 91

10.10.10.10 (Suggested tunes: EVENTIDE;
MORECAMBE; TOULON)

Deep in the shelter of the Lord I dwell,
 And in the shadow of God's love abide;
No pestilence or snare will me assail,
 When God Almighty watches at my side.

Beneath God's hov'ring wings I rest secure,
 With calm assurance that my help is near;
God's loving-kindness my protection sure,
 And e'er attends to banish all my fear.

Since I have made the Lord my dwelling place,
 Home of my care and harbor for my praise;
Great hosts of angels, messengers of grace,
 God sends to keep me safe in all my ways.

"For I, the Lord, have bound you safe in love,
 You need not fear, I will your rescue be";
Since You, O Lord, from danger me remove,
 My song shall be Your praise eternally.

Psalm 92

LM (Suggested tunes: OLD HUNDREDTH; TALLIS' CANON;
DUKE STREET)

How good to bring our thanks to God!
  To sing the praises of our Lord!
Each rising day, God's steadfast love
  Like finest oil on us is poured.

Your faithfulness I sing by night;
  My songs of joy with darkness clad;
Your music, Lord, is my delight,
  And all Your works have made me glad.

The righteous in God's courts shall grow
  And flourish while they have their breath;
The God who sees their righteous days
  Will not forsake them after death.

Psalm 93

LM (Suggested tunes: BOURBON; DEO GRACIAS;
WINCHESTER NEW)

The Lord is clad in majesty,
    Adorned in glorious array;
The throne which earth's wide bounds ordained
    Still wears the crown of God today.

The pillars of creation stand,
    Unshaken in their ageless flight;
The raging floods their wrath dispel,
    And meekly wane before God's might.

Your testimonies, Lord, are fast;
    In holiness, Your house secure;
From age to age shall Your decrees
    In righteousness and truth endure.

Psalm 94

SM (Suggested tunes: ST. MICHAEL; ST. THOMAS;
FESTAL SONG)

Arise, O Judge of earth,
    Enthroned above the clouds;
Send vengeance to the wicked lot;
    Humiliate the proud!

They boast, "God does not see
    The truth behind our lies!
The poor, the needy count for naught,
    As chaff before our eyes."

But You, who gave us ears,
    Will not refuse to hear;
Who gave us eyes will not be blind,
    Nor slow to shed a tear.

O teach Your law, O Lord,
    That I may live aright;
Chastise me when I go astray;
    Uphold me by Your might.

The steadfast love of God
    Is mine till life is past;
To guide my steps across the years,
    And bring me home at last.

Psalm 95

8.7.8.7.8.8.7 (Suggested tunes: MIT FREUDEN ZART;
ALLEIN GOTT IN DER HOH')

Come, let us sing unto the Lord,
    The Rock of our salvation;
May we rejoice in songs of praise
    Before the God of creation,
By whose design the earth was planned;
The seas were filled at Your command,
    O God of ev'ry nation.

Come, let us praise the Lord of lords,
    Who brings us life and pleasure;
A Shepherd who attends the flock
    With care that none can measure.
Give us desire to hear Your voice;
The will to make Your way our choice;
    Your love our fondest treasure.

Psalm 96

CMD (Suggested tunes: ELLACOMBE; ALL SAINTS NEW; KINGSFOLD)

O sing new songs unto the Lord,
    With shouts God's name adore;
Proclaim salvation day by day,
    God's glory evermore!
Our God to whom all voices rise
    Is worthy of our praise;
Who formed the earth beneath our feet,
    The sun to light our days.

All lesser idols fade away,
    As wisdom intercedes;
The greatest feats our minds conceive
    Are pale beside God's deeds.
O heav'ns, be glad; O earth, rejoice!
    Your deeds and praise accord
To God, and with creation sing
    The glories of the Lord.

Psalm 97

SMD (Suggested tunes: DIADEMATA; TERRA BEATA;
ST. THOMAS)

God reigns! Let earth rejoice!
    Let oceans shout God's might!
Borne up by truth and righteousness,
    God's throne is our delight.
God's fire ignites the clouds
    With judgment swift and just;
The evil find their deeds in vain;
    God's foes are brought to dust.

Vict'ry to those who bow
    In awe before God's sword;
Who place their strong reliance in
    The promise of God's Word.
False idols rise to claim
    The weakness of our pride,
But cannot touch the faithful ones,
    For God stands at our side.

All who would seek the right,
    And evil things deplore,
Find pleasure in the courts of God,
    And comfort evermore.
The radiance of God's light
    Beams joy into our days;
Filled with the glory of God's love,
    Our hearts resound with praise.

Psalm 98

8.7.8.7 D (Suggested tunes: BEACH SPRING; HOLY MANNA;
AUSTRIAN HYMN)

Sing new songs to God Almighty,
    Marvel at God's majesty!
In the face of foes around us
    God has brought us victory!
Nations all shall see God's promise;
    Love endure and faith prevail;
Evermore will God be gracious
    To the house of Israel.

Joyful songs of praise and honor
    Earth shall sing with one accord;
Horn and trumpet raise a mighty
    Shout of tribute to our Lord!
Seas and floods rejoice with gladness;
    All the earth God's gifts profess:
Endless grace conceived in mercy,
    Justice born in righteousness.

Psalm 99

6.6.8.4 D (Suggested tune: LEONI)

God reigns, enthroned on high;
    Let all the earth proclaim
With trembling lips the awesome might
    Of God's great name!
A holy Lord, whose rule
    Is marked with equity;
Whose righteousness to us is bound
    All time to be.

Unto the priests of old
    Who called upon God's name,
The Law was spoken from the clouds,
    And wrought in flame!
To God's commands give heed;
    In faith, endure always;
Let Zion's walls forever ring
    With songs of praise!

Psalm 100

LM (Suggested tunes: OLD HUNDREDTH; DUKE STREET; PUER NOBIS NASCITUR)

Let ev'ry voice on earth resound,
    And joyful hearts hold God adored;
In gladness may God's courts abound
    With songs of praise unto the Lord.

You are the Lord; by whose design
    All we in nature claim our place;
Your flock, we bind our lives to You,
    And rest secure beneath Your grace.

Before the Lord bring thanks and praise,
    Unfathomed mercies wait in store;
God's goodness blesses all our days,
    God's truth endures for evermore!

Psalm 101

CM (Suggested tunes: DUNDEE; ST. FLAVIAN; ST. PETER)

Of loyalty and justice, Lord,
  My song shall ever be.
If I pursue the blameless way,
  When will You come to me?

My house, my heart, become the place
  Integrity resides;
For evil finds no shelter where
  The truth of God abides.

From willful pride and base deceit
  My spirit far remove;
That I may dwell in faith secure,
  And flourish in Your love.

Psalm 102

SM (Suggested tunes: ST. BRIDE; SOUTHWELL; ST. MICHAEL)

Hear now my prayer, O Lord,
    I cry on bended knee,
That in the hour of utmost need,
    Your presence sets me free.

My tears have been my drink,
    With ashes for my bread;
Your anger does my life consume,
    And give me up for dead.

But God in glory reigns
    With grace as well as fire;
To judge with pity and to save
    Is God's supreme desire.

Let Zion be a home
    To those who hold her dear,
That people yet unborn may know
    Their Lord is ever near.

The heav'ns some day shall pass,
    And earth return to sod,
But coming years will see no end
    To love which comes from God.

A PSALM OF THANKSGIVING

Psalm 103

7.7.7.7.7.7 (Suggested tunes: REDHEAD 76; DIX; RATISBON)

Bless, O bless the Lord, my soul,
　　All within me, praise the Lord!
In the fullness of my life,
　　Ever is God's name adored!
Who redeems my sinful soul,
Makes my fainting spirit whole.

Merciful, with grace endued,
　　God will judge with righteousness;
Slow to anger or to chide,
　　Swift to pardon and to bless.
Though our sin deserves the rod,
More than sparing is our God.

High as heav'n above the earth
　　Is the Lord's redeeming love;
Far as east from west is laid,
　　So does God our sin remove.
As a parent, pity take;
Cleanse our hearts for Your own sake.

Like the grass that grows and fades,
　　So the cycle of our days;
But God's love is ever sure
　　Unto those who sing God's praise.
Lord of heav'n, in faithfulness
May I never cease to bless.

Psalm 104a

SMD (Suggested tunes: DIADEMATA; TERRA BEATA; ST. THOMAS)

O bless the Lord, my soul,
  With might and honor clad;
Who makes the darkest midnight bright,
  The mourning spirit glad.
The heav'ns become God's robe,
  God's brow the stars adorn;
The fire and flame, like messengers,
  On wings of wind are borne.

Earth at God's word was formed,
  And seas the land did drown;
As footstools, hills arose to meet
  The peaks that framed God's crown.
God speaks; the raging flood
  Deserts the fertile plain;
And nevermore its bounds exceeds
  To smother earth again.

Who can recount the good
  God's hands for us have done;
We day to day rehearse God's deeds,
  Yet they have just begun.
Let sinners be consumed
  In their own vanity,
Unless they know their sure defeat,
  And claim their victory.

Psalm 104b

CM (Suggested tunes: ST. PETER; LAND OF REST;
ST. STEPHEN)

O Lord, how marvelous Your works;
    Your wisdom, without peer!
The richest blessings heav'n can boast
    You deign to show us here.

The sea is filled from shore to shore
    With creatures great and small;
The minnows teem the tide with whales;
    God's care extends to all.

They wait for God to give them food,
    Who dwell across the land;
And in the season of God's grace
    They feed from God's own hand.

The absence of the Lord gives rise
    To stubborn, faithless fears;
God's Spirit, feeble life renews;
    God's breath can dry our tears.

Your glory, Lord, always endures,
    Your mercy, all our days;
O may I never cease to fill
    Your courts with songs of praise!

Psalm 105a

CMD (Suggested tunes: ELLACOMBE; KINGSFOLD)

Sing songs of praise and thanks to God,
    Who wondrous deeds has done;
By whose design was life ordained,
    God's strength, the battle won.
The judgments of the Lord are just;
    Earth moves beneath God's voice;
The righteous glory in God's might,
    And faithful hearts rejoice.

Remember well when God's elect
    In bondage bore the chains,
Endured the test of faith and won
    God's favor yet again.
These slaves, redeemed through true belief,
    The tyrant's rod destroyed;
They claimed the blessings of the land
    Which masters once enjoyed.

Psalm 105b

CM (Suggested tunes: Land of Rest; Tallis' Ordinal;
St. Flavian)

Rejoice, you faithful, in the Lord,
    A song of thanks now raise;
For all the goodness to us giv'n,
    Unite to sing God's praise.

The miracles God's grace fulfills
    Are wrought for our avail;
How blessed are they whose hearts confirm
    God's love will never fail!

The just rewards of unbelief
    Are fashioned through our fears;
And nightmares, once imagined, gain
    Their flesh when doubt appears.

But to the stalwart in their faith
    God's blessings are displayed;
They sing with joy, the chosen ones
    Whose hope in God is stayed.

Psalm 106

CM (Suggested tunes: ST. STEPHEN; ST. ANNE; ST. MAGNUS)

Our gracious Lord be always praised,
    Give thanks to God above;
The blessings we enjoy on earth
    Are gifts of God's great love.

Remember, Lord, our faithfulness,
    When in Your courts we meet;
May our degree of righteousness
    Find mercy at Your feet.

The chosen ones, from bondage freed,
    Were sheltered in Your fold;
With hands unmoistened by the sea,
    They cast an ox of gold.

The righteous remnant of their tribe
    From sin found liberty;
When my own judgment shall be due,
    Be gracious unto me.

BOOK V

Psalm 107

11.11.11.11 (Suggested tune: O QUANTA QUALIA)

Give thanks to God,
   Who all goodness has brought us;
God, whose great love
Shall redeem us forever;
From earth's wide corners,
   God's mercy has sought us;
May God's redemption
Depart from us never.

Hear when we call from
   Amid desolation,
Starving for life,
Yet more frightened of living;
When You, O Lord,
   Offer true consolation,
Let us respond
With a song of thanksgiving.

Hear us, the pris'ners
   Of sin and affliction,
Fast bound in shackles
Of doubt and misgiving;
When You, O Lord,
   Offer strength to conviction,
Let us respond
With a song of thanksgiving.

Hear when the earth
   In its rage would destroy us;
Wind and the sea
Steal our passion for living.
When quiet shelter
   And love You provide us,
Let us respond
With a song of thanksgiving.

Psalm 108

CM (Suggested tunes: MORNING SONG; AZMON; MCKEE)

My heart, O God, is now attuned
　　To offer songs of praise!
Awake, my soul, the dawn resounds
　　With joy throughout my days!

O may my tongue be never still
　　To speak my grateful part
To God, who reigns above the clouds,
　　Yet dwells within my heart.

Exalt Yourself above the sky,
　　And shower me with light,
That where the faithful find their rest,
　　I, too, may sleep the night.

The lands of earth to You belong,
　　The desert and the plain;
Reclaim them for Your kingdom now,
　　And bring me home again.

Psalm 109

8.7.8.7 D (Suggested tunes: Nettleton; Holy Manna;
Pleading Savior)

Be not silent, God of judgment,
    When my foes against me rail;
For I know their hate will perish,
    And Your righteousness prevail.
In return for love, they curse me;
    At my constant faith, deride;
I can bear their accusations,
    If You, Lord, stand at my side.

Help me, Lord, in my affliction;
    In Your steadfast love I stand;
When You bring to me salvation,
    Vengeance, too, is by Your hand.
With my mouth, I'll sing Your praises;
    With my heart, Your love confess;
Crown my life with Your affection;
    Let me live Your name to bless.

Psalm 110

LM (Suggested tunes: DUKE STREET; DEO GRACIAS; WAREHAM)

Thus spoke the Lord, "I will defend
    The righteous, who at my right hand
Subdue their foes beneath their feet,
    And all their wicked threats withstand."

God shall send forth from Zion's hill
    A mighty scepter to their throne,
That they who rule in righteousness
    Shall never face their foes alone.

How great the pow'r of God to bless;
    Heav'ns richest gifts on us to pour;
God's wrath may shatter disbelief,
    But faith is ours for evermore.

Psalm 111

8.7.8.7.8.7 (Suggested tunes: REGENT SQUARE; WESTMINSTER ABBEY)

With my heart, I praise my Maker;
    Ever in God's temple sing;
Great and glorious are God's mercies,
    Endless honor shall we bring
To the Lord; let all creation
    With great adoration ring!

God, all gracious and all caring,
    Send Your blessings from above;
If in wrath Your arm works vengeance,
    Can Your heart with pity move?
May our sins by grace inherit
    Justice tempered with Your love.

All Your laws are sure established,
    Wrought of love and equity;
And the promise of Your mercy
    Shall endure all time to be.
Those whose lips sing of Your glory
    Evermore Your face shall see.

Psalm 112

10.10.11.11 (Suggested tunes: LYONS; HANOVER;
LAUDATE DOMINUM)

How happy are they, whose eager delight
    Is none but to praise and serve God aright;
Who make, Lord, Your will their unquestioned decree,
    And nurture their children Your children to be.

Forever the Lord will honor the race
    Which worships in awe, and prospers in grace;
In darkness, the godly a radiance shall find,
    And equal compassion for those who are kind.

In presence of foes, the just will not fear,
    For peace is God's vow, and ever is near;
To those who in confidence rest on God's will,
    God's unmeasured mercies their vict'ry fulfill.

From bountiful stores, God's generous hand
    Shall scatter its good far over the land;
The poor shall inherit the wealth of the proud,
    And tongues of the righteous sing praises aloud!

Psalm 113

8.7.8.7 D (Suggested tunes: ABBOT'S LEIGH; HYFRYDOL;
BEACH SPRING)

Bless the Lord, O saints and servants,
　　Praise the might of God's great name;
Ageless, matchless, filled with wonder,
　　Yesterday, today, the same.
When the dawn receives the sunrise
　　Till the night returns its rays,
Shall the glory of God's goodness
　　Be the theme of all our praise.

Who in heav'n can be God's equal?
　　Who on earth with God compare?
Who can raise the poor from ashes,
　　Lift the needy from despair?
God alone invites the helpless
　　With the strong to share reward;
Fields once barren yield a harvest,
　　Tongues once silent praise their Lord.

A HYMN OF PRAISE TO GOD

Psalm 114

7.7.7.7 (Suggested tunes: AUS DER TIEFE; NUN KOMM,
DER HEIDEN HEILAND)

When the bonds of God's elect
    Shattered were by God's own hand;
Judah's house became a throne,
    Israel, God's chosen land.

At their feet, the sea withdrew;
    Through the tides they safely passed;
Hills and mountains skipped as lambs,
    Long in exile, home at last.

Why do earth's dominions shake,
    Floods subside, and shackles fall?
Why, indeed? Like us, they know
    Jacob's God is Lord of all.

Psalm 115

SM (Suggested tunes: ST. MICHAEL; ST. THOMAS;
FESTAL SONG)

Not unto us, O Lord,
    But let all glory be
A tribute for Your mercy's sake,
    And truth eternally.

The faithless will inquire,
    "Where may our God be found?"
They blindly seek a god of gold;
    We see You all around.

Their idols, like their faith,
    Hold emptiness and pride;
And in their quest for greater gods,
    These soon are cast aside.

But Israel's faith is stayed,
    In Aaron's God secure;
An everlasting help and shield
    Is God, our refuge sure.

The Lord who lights the stars
    And spins the earth in space
Shall bless us with untold delights,
    And nurture us with grace.

Psalm 116

LM (Suggested tunes: ROCKINGHAM; ERHALT UNS,
HERR; CONDITOR ALME SIDERUM)

I love the Lord, who heard my voice
    And answered my most earnest prayer;
When snares of death my life would take,
    You lift me, God, from my despair.

O what can I to good return
    For all the bounty from Your store?
Seen with such grace, my highest prize
    Is naught; what can I give You more?

I lift salvation's cup from which
    You had me drink to seal my vow;
And in the sight of all around,
    I honor my commitment now.

The recompense for what is mine
    Is to exalt Your name always;
My heart with thanks should ne'er run dry,
    Nor tongue refuse to sing Your praise.

Psalm 117

CM (Suggested tunes: McKee; St. Anne; Azmon)

Rejoice in God, you nations all,
    Let tongues God's might record;
For great beyond our fondest dreams
    Are blessings of the Lord.

God's steadfast love is unsurpassed
    By our imagined worth;
God's faithfulness shall far outlive
    The timeless bounds of earth.

Psalm 118

8.7.8.7.8.8.7 (Suggested tunes: MIT FREUDEN ZART;
NUN FREUT EUCH)

Give thanks unto our gracious God,
   Whose love endures forever;
The Lord, our strength and song shall be,
   From whom no fault can sever.
Sing mighty songs of victory,
Both now and for eternity,
   For God will leave us never.

I shall not die, but I shall live,
   And sing God's grace with elation;
Though I deserve no more than death,
   God blesses me with salvation.
The gate that should unyielding be
Is open wide to welcome me,
   Give thanks and adoration!

Upon the stones the builders judged
   Imperfect, weak and tender,
Now rest the corners of God's house,
   Still unsurpassed in splendor.
This is the day the Lord has made;
God is my sun, and God my shade;
   Rejoice, and praise gladly render!

Psalm 119a

CM (Suggested tunes: LAND OF REST; ST. PETER;
WINCHESTER OLD)

How blessed are they whose path is pure,
    Who keep God's Law aright;
And happy they who by true faith
    Find favor in God's sight.

The Lord commands that holy Law
    Should be our constant guide;
And those who bow to God's decree
    Shall not be cast aside.

O may we ever steadfast be
    In living out God's will;
Whose Law, our counsel will remain;
    Whose love, our comfort still.

Psalm 119b

LM (Suggested tunes: Kedron; Rockingham Old;
Erhalt Uns, Herr)

Through faith, O God, the young, the old,
　　Find treasure in divine decree;
In every word, Your voice is heard,
　　Proclaiming who we ought to be.

What richer gift, what finer fare,
　　Can we imagine or proclaim
Than holy Light, forever bright,
　　Shed on our path in Your dear Name?

Teach us Your laws, that we may live
　　As children in Your tender care;
Help us to know, where'er we go,
　　Your peace, and grace, and love are there.

Psalm 119c

LM (Suggested tunes: Wareham; Bourbon; Winchester New)

Teach me, O Lord, Your holy Law;
    The will to follow so impart
That I with understanding may
    Observe it with a faithful heart.

Let Your right path be ever mine,
    For in Your precepts I delight;
May selfish gain and empty pride
    Be turned away and put to flight.

Grant us the passion to embrace
    Your constant will amid all strife;
For faith unfalt'ring, grant us grace;
    For righteousness, eternal life.

Psalm 119d

LM (Suggested tunes: WAREHAM; BOURBON;
WINCHESTER NEW)

O Lord, how I adore Your Law,
    The greatest treasure for the least!
It is to me a banquet spread
    Where my most hungry thoughts may feast.

Who in Your Word shall meditate
    Finds truth in heart, and hope in tears;
The wisdom which Your Law imparts
    Outlasts the number of our years.

Withhold my feet from evil snares,
    And keep them on the path less trod;
For sweet Your words unto my mouth,
    And true the precepts of my God!

Psalm 119e

LM (Suggested tunes: WINCHESTER NEW; O WALY WALY;
PUER NOBIS NASCITUR)

Your Word, O Lord, a lamp shall be
　To guide my feet, to light my way;
The darkest path unto my prize
　By Your rich grace is bright as day.

Revive, O God, this fainting soul;
　Remain my stay amid distress;
Teach me Your law, that I may live
　A life renewed in righteousness.

My heritage, Your lasting word,
　Which through the years is ever sure;
May I reflect Your constant love,
　And know Your truth shall long endure.

Psalm 119f

LM (Suggested tunes: OLD HUNDREDTH;
PUER NOBIS NASCITUR; WINCHESTER NEW)

Give light and understanding, Lord,
　　To us who live to keep Your Word;
May songs of gratitude proclaim
　　Our joy for all Your love conferred.

Amid injustice and deceit,
　　Show us deliv'rance from our fears;
Let righteousness become the rule
　　To guide our lives, and dry our tears.

Be present, God, with all who seek
　　To follow every step You trace;
Keep us illumined by Your law,
　　And steadfast in Your saving grace.

Psalm 119g

7.6.7.6 D (Suggested tunes: Aurelia; Llangloffan;
Valet Will Ich Dir Geben)

Lord, You are righteous always;
    Your judgments, all are wise.
And faithful is the witness
    Which stands before our eyes.
My fervent zeal consumes me,
    O let me never cease
To hold You in remembrance,
    And in Your Word find peace.

Your Word, so pure and holy,
    Is more than life to me;
When strength may fade within me,
    How great my love will be!
From age to age, Your justice
    Our saving health assures;
And righteousness, with mercy,
    From age to age endures.

Psalm 120

LM (Suggested tunes: WINCHESTER NEW; BOURBON; GERMANY)

In my distress, I cried to God,
    "From vain deceit, Lord, rescue me;
Let not the threats sharp tongues may speak
    Defy the faith that makes me free.

Too long has war encompassed me,
    Contention raging without cease;
Help me, amid the conflict, be
    A constant symbol of Your peace."

Psalm 121

LM (Suggested tunes: PUER NOBIS NASCITUR;
O WALY WALY; DUKE STREET)

I lift my eyes unto the hills;
    From where shall come my help at last?
Whate'er the need, God will provide,
    The Lord, by whom the world was cast.

Each day God is a strength and shield
    Against the onslaught of my foes;
And to the dangers of the night,
    The eyes of God are never closed.

The promise of the Lord is sure:
    To hold me in unyielding care;
Throughout my life, may faith confirm
    That where I am, the Lord is there.

Psalm 122

7.6.7.6 D (Suggested tunes: EWING; MUNICH)

How glad was my rejoicing,
    How great my soul's delight,
When into God's own temple
    My friends did me invite!
Long have my feet been planted
    Within the city gates;
And soon I'll claim the promise
    For which my spirit waits.

Jerusalem, the city
    Where tribes are joined as one,
Where God's elect find justice,
    Where righteousness is done;
And I, a child of David
    And heir to God's decree,
Shall take the place in glory
    That God prepares for me.

Jerusalem, God's city,
    May peace dwell in your walls;
And those who love you prosper,
    Whatever else befalls;
Within your vaulted towers,
    Secure I take my rest;
At peace with God's assurance,
    And with God's favor blessed.

Psalm 123

CM (Suggested tunes: St. Flavian; Morning Song; Dundee)

I lift my eyes to You, O Lord,
    Your throne, earth's canopy;
As masters hold their servants dear,
    So, Lord, remember me.

More like a child than bonded slave,
    I claim Your grace outright;
The proud shall fall, but yet the meek
    Find favor in Your sight.

Your boundless mercies, Lord, outweigh
    The scorn we must endure;
While foes shall fade in their contempt,
    Your love will long endure.

Psalm 124

CM (Suggested tunes: ST. ANNE; MORNING SONG;
ST. PETER)

If God had not been on our side,
    When wars around us rose;
Who would have been the sure defense
    Against our mortal foes?

Their anger at our presence raged;
    Their wrath, a swelling tide,
To draw us underneath the flood,
    Were God not at our side.

The Lord be praised, at whose right hand
    Our enemies are stayed;
Our lasting shield, the name of God,
    Who heav'n and earth has made.

Psalm 125

8.7.8.7 D (Suggested tunes: Beach Spring; Hyfrydol; Holy Manna)

Those who place on God reliance
    In despair shall not be moved;
As the mountains hug the valley,
    So embraced are God's beloved.
Everlasting is Mount Zion,
    From creation's dawn till night;
And eternal is God's promise
    Unto those who live aright.

All good blessings shall be given
    To the servants of God's will;
Just rewards and retributions,
    Once conferred, are with us still.
Those who work against God's healing
    Have their ill with ill repaid;
But the faithful of the kingdom
    Find their full redemption made.

Psalm 126

8.7.8.7 D (Suggested tunes: IN BABILONE; HOLY MANNA;
BEACH SPRING)

When the Lord brought home our treasure,
　　All delights were like a dream;
In defeat, a shout of vict'ry;
　　In the sand, a flowing stream.
Mouths that once were parched with anguish
　　Now with shouts of joy are filled;
Laughter now displaces sadness
　　For the goodness God has willed.

Bring us back to former glory,
　　Lost through years of exile's pain;
Generations long forgotten
　　Seek God's favor to regain.
Those who plant their seeds with grieving,
　　Wetting soil with falling tears,
Shall rejoice in time of harvest,
　　Reaping hope for all their years.

Psalm 127

CMD (Suggested tunes: KINGSFOLD; MORNING SONG)

Except the house is built by God,
    Its stones for naught are laid;
The city, without God's defense,
    Is feeble and afraid.
To eat the bread of anxious toil
    Makes all our labor vain;
God feeds our cherished souls with rest
    To face our work again.

In every age, the greatest gifts
    God's fullness can accord
Are generations born to claim
    The blessings of the Lord.
The ancient die, the young grow old;
    They, too, shall fade away;
Creation, as God's heritage,
    Begins with each new day.

Psalm 128

8.7.8.7.8.7 (Suggested tunes: REGENT SQUARE;
WESTMINSTER ABBEY)

Blessed are they whose adoration
    Of the Lord with awe is filled;
All the good wrought by their labor
    Is their gain, so God has willed.
Righteous minds, infused with justice;
    Steadfast hearts, with love instilled.

Like a fruitful vine they flourish,
    Branches of a shelt'ring tree,
So shall children's children gather
    At God's table faithfully;
Prayers replete with peace and blessing
    Rise for all eternity.

Psalm 129

SM (Suggested tunes: St. Thomas; Festal Song; Southwell)

How fervently my foes
    Have fought me from my youth,
Yet their deceit cannot defeat
    God's all-sustaining truth.

They plow their furrows deep,
    And turn my flesh for sod;
Despite their rush, they will not crush
    My constant faith in God.

Let them receive their due,
    According to God's word;
And in their place, confirm through grace,
    The blessings of the Lord.

Psalm 130

7.7.7.7 D (Suggested tunes: Aberstwyth; Nun Komm,
Der Heiden Heiland)

From the depths I cry to You,
    Savior, Lord, my prayer receive;
Who can stand the press of sin?
    Those who in Your grace believe.
Mark not my iniquity,
    Lest the burden break my heart;
Not my heart alone, but Yours;
    In your mercy, bear my part.

For the Lord my soul awaits;
    In God's word, my hope is laid;
As the sentries by the dawn
    For their patience are repaid.
Hope in God, O Israel;
    God, whose steadfast love is sure;
Who for us redemption brings;
    God, whose mercies shall endure.

Psalm 131

LM (Suggested tunes: ROCKINGHAM; CANONBURY;
CONDITOR ALME SIDERUM)

O Lord, my heart is not too high,
    Nor do my eyes look far above
The things which You for me appoint,
    Except to hope for Your great love.

A child again in mother's arms,
    My soul at peace in Your accord;
I fix my confidence and hope
    In tender mercies of the Lord.

Psalm 132

7.7.7.7 (Suggested tunes: AUS DER TIEFE; SONG 13;
NUN KOMM; DER HEIDEN HEILAND)

Call to mind, O Lord, the pain;
    Hardships David did endure;
That Your dwelling place should be
    In his heart forever sure.

Come, O God, and dwell in me;
    Clothe my soul in righteousness;
May Your presence know my joy,
    May my pleasure be to bless.

You have promised worthy heirs
    Will inherit Zion's throne;
Who with truth and justice rule,
    And confess You Lord alone.

You, O Lord, all good extend;
    To my needs Your care provide;
So be in my life that I
    After death with You abide.

Psalm 133

LM (Suggested tunes: TALLIS' CANON;
CONDITOR ALME SIDERUM; CANONBURY)

How good when all the earth is one,
  And hearts embrace community;
When strife will cease to separate,
  And love binds all in unity.

As oil anointed Aaron's head,
  And dew adorns the mountainside,
So peace and blessing of the Lord
  Within the faithful heart abide.

Psalm 134

CM (Suggested tunes: LAND OF REST; IRISH;
MORNING SONG)

Come, bless the Lord, you servants all,
    Who in God's house by night
Bring to the Lord the highest praise,
    And to the darkness, light.

Lift up your hands unto the Lord,
    In confidence secure,
Though earth and heaven pass away,
    God's goodness shall endure.

Psalm 135

7.6.7.6 D (Suggested tunes: ELLACOMBE; LANCASHIRE;
VALET WILL ICH DIR GEBEN)

O praise God's name together,
　　You servants of the Lord;
O Lord, for all Your favor
　　To us, You are adored!
Within Your holy temple,
　　Before Your sacred throne,
The chosen heirs of Jacob
　　Proclaim You God alone!

O Lord, no mind can measure
　　The greatness of Your might;
You gave the earth its orbit,
　　And set the stars to flight.
The clouds You raised in heaven
　　Give to the fields their rain;
Your Word lifts waves from oceans,
　　And mountains from the plain.

False gods may rise before us,
　　Their vanity display;
But as the hands that made them,
　　They, too, shall fade away.
Your Name, O God Almighty,
　　Endures for endless days;
And newborn generations
　　Unite to sing Your praise.

Psalm 136

7.7.7.7.7.7 (Suggested tunes: REDHEAD 76; DIX; RATISBON)

O give thanks unto the Lord,
    Who above all gods shall reign;
Sing your praise with one accord,
    Ever in God's fold remain.
For God's steadfast love is sure,
    And forever shall endure!

Praise the wonder of God's might,
    Who the earth and seas displayed;
God, who brought to darkness light,
    In whose image, we are made.
For God's steadfast love is sure,
    And forever shall endure!

More than our imagined grace
    Are the mercies of our God;
Hope is ours, if we but place
    Our reliance in God's Word.
For God's steadfast love is sure,
    And forever shall endure!

Psalm 137

7.7.7.7 D (Suggested tunes: ABERSTWYTH; NUN KOMM;
DER HEIDEN HEILAND)

By the streams of Babylon
    Wept the nation Israel;
Harps hung mute on willow boughs;
    Tears from captive eyelids fell.
"Sing us one of Zion's songs!"
    Our tormentors mocked our grief;
How can we as strangers here
    Bow before their unbelief?

If Jerusalem should fade
    From my fondest thoughts, I pray.
Let my strength alike disperse,
    And my tongue become as clay.
To abide within God's walls
    Is the greatest joy to me;
Vanquish those who scorn God's throne;
    From their tumult, set me free.

Psalm 138

6.6.6.6.8.8 (Suggested tune: DARWALL'S 148TH)

O Lord, my heart will sing,
   I give You thanks and praise,
And in Your holy temple bow
   Throughout my days.
Your steadfast faithfulness and love,
   O God, let shower from above.

God answered when I called,
   Responding to my need;
The rulers of the earth shall name
   You Lord indeed!
The proud will fall, their boasts are vain,
   The meek of earth shall o'er them reign.

Though dangers gather round,
   O, Lord, preserve my life;
And by Your strong and forceful arm
   I conquer strife.
God will give heed, my hopes fulfill,
   And keep the vow to love me still.

Psalm 139

8.7.8.7 D (Suggested tunes: HYFRYDOL; ABBOT'S LEIGH;
BEACH SPRING)

You, O Lord, have searched and known me,
    When I rest, and when I rise;
Not a single thought I cherish
    Is kept secret from Your eyes.
Ev'ry word my lips would murmur
    Needs no speech to make it known;
All I do, ere it be started,
    Is as done to You alone.

Whither shall I flee Your Spirit?
    From Your presence, vanish where?
Heights of heaven, darkest shadows
    Hide me not, for You are there.
If I take the wings of morning,
    and in earth's far corner stand;
Even there Your love will find me,
    Hold me fast within Your hand.

In the brilliance of Your glory,
    Darkest night is bright as day;
Shadows flee the path before me,
    When Your wisdom lights my way.
You who knit my parts together,
    Knew my life before my birth,
Sees my faults, esteems my promise
    Far beyond my feeble worth.

Lord, how precious is Your favor
    Shown in such goodwill to me;
To the godless in their rancor,
    Let me Your confessor be.
Search, O Lord, my heart's ambitions,
    Thoughts my mouth would dare not say;
Judge with mercy, and preserve me
    In the everlasting way.

Psalm 140

7.7.7.7 (Suggested tunes: Aus Der Tiefe; Nun Komm;
Der Heiden Heiland; Song 13)

From destructive threats, O Lord,
　From the evil all around,
Let Your strength my soul preserve,
　Refuge in Your arms be found.

Like a serpent, would they strike,
　Sharp against Your servant's heel;
Fierce are they who force my fate,
　Fortune, life, and faith would steal.

Yet I know, You are my God,
　Who has seen me through distress;
My salvation, You will send
　Vict'ry for my righteousness.

Ever shall the Lord supply
　Goodness as our needs demand;
Through God's justice, by God's grace,
　May we in God's presence stand.

Psalm 141

4.10.10.10.4 (Suggested tune: ORA LABORA)

I cry to God;
Make haste to hear me,
   Lord, on You I call;
In my distress,
   You are my all in all.
My prayer ascends as
   Incense to the sky;
   My hope is nigh.

May I be pure;
Guard me from evil;
   Let my lips proclaim
My sure salvation
   In Your holy name.
So guide my footsteps
   On Your sheltered ways
   Through all my days.

Psalm 142

8.6.8.6.8.6 (Suggested tunes: MORNING SONG; CORONATION)

Unto my God I cried aloud,
　　My supplication poured;
In my distress, God heard my prayer;
　　My fainting soul restored.
The deepest valleys of my life
　　Are plains before the Lord.

Around me camp the hosts of death,
　　Who would my path assail;
None but the Lord stands at my side,
　　And none but God prevail.
Therefore, my Lord, I trust in You,
　　Whose promise will not fail.

O save me from their raging hate,
　　Which would my faith destroy;
Before the wiles of their deceit,
　　Your saving grace employ,
That I may find my heart's delight,
　　And revel in Your joy!

Psalm 143

7.8.7.8.8.8 (Suggested tune: LIEBSTER JESU)

To my prayer, Lord, bend Your ear;
 Faithful in Your vow to hear me.
Let Your righteousness pronounce
 Such a judgment as would cheer me.
None is worthy of Your favor,
But by grace Your mercy savor.

You who in the ancient past
 Wrought great deeds for our salvation;
Take our outstretched hands in Yours,
 Lift us from our desolation.
Help me, for my spirit fails;
Only Your rich love prevails.

As the morning claims the dawn,
 Light appears to quell night's blindness;
In the radiance of Your face,
 Bathe me with Your loving-kindness.
Fill me with the sacred leaven
That will raise my soul to heaven.

Psalm 144

8.7.8.7 D (Suggested tunes: EBENEZER; IN BABILONE; BEACH SPRING)

Blessed be God, who is my fortress,
　By whose hand my own is led;
Those who would my life endanger
　Shall themselves be lost instead.
What am I that God should prosper
　Me with righteousness always?
Turn the boasts of my ambitions
　Into heartfelt songs of praise.

Stretch Your hand, O my Redeemer,
　Rescue me from hostile plight;
With Your sword, a blazing pattern
　Slash across my darkest night.
Then will I new songs of vict'ry
　Sing to You, who at my side
Brought my foes to their destruction,
　Swept them up in their own pride.

Happy those who claim Your mercy,
　Blessed are they who know Your love;
Sons and daughters, strong and vibrant,
　In Your wisdom live and move.
May our lives be such to merit
　Some degree of all Your store;
In Your house, may we find favor
　And abide for evermore.

Psalm 145

8.7.8.7 D (Suggested tunes: HYFRYDOL; ABBOT'S LEIGH;
BEECHER; BEACH SPRING)

I will ever sing Your praises,
    For all time, Your name I'll bless;
Without peer is Your great glory,
    Limitless Your righteousness.
Each new generation numbers
    All Your blessings as their own;
To the earth's most far-flung regions
    Is Your majesty made known.

You are gracious, full of mercy,
    Slow to anger, quick to love;
Saints below may glimpse Your kingdom
    In the lofty skies above.
In this life, the best I savor
    Is but common fare to me;
All the riches earth can harvest
    Cannot match Your majesty.

For the Lord is ever faithful
    To supply our deepest need;
Justice grows from every judgment,
    Wholesome bread from every seed.
God is ne'er too far to hear us,
    Never deaf to our demands;
Those who love and trust the promise
    Rest secure within God's hand.

Psalm 146

8.7.8.7 D (Suggested tunes: ABBOT'S LEIGH; BEECHER;
NETTLETON)

Bless the Lord, give praise and honor
    Unto God who lends me breath;
May my tongue God's greatness never
    Cease to tell before my death.
And in songs of sovereign goodness,
    Let me sing beyond the grave;
God, whose grace my life to ransom,
    God, whose will my soul to save.

Blessed are they whose hope is vested
    In the God of Israel;
In the hour of deepest anguish,
    God's provisions will not fail;
Freedom for the shackled spirit,
    Strength and stay to those who fall;
Blessings offered without measure,
    Righteousness enough for all.

Psalm 147a

10.10.10.4 (Suggested tunes: ENGELBERG;
SINE NOMINE with extra Alleluia)

Praise to the Lord, for it is good to praise
God, who the loving heart with love repays;
Whose gracious kindness blesses us always,
   Alleluia!

God makes the broken heart rejoice once more;
A healing ointment on our wounds will pour;
Our feeble spirits shall the Lord restore,
   Alleluia!

Great is the Lord, abundant in the care
Provided for all creatures everywhere;
To God's rich love, no earthly loves compare,
   Alleluia!

Our greatest strength is weakness in God's sight;
In our ambitions, God does not delight,
But for our constant will to live aright,
   Alleluia!

Psalm 147b

8.7.8.7.8.7 (Suggested tunes: WESTMINSTER ABBEY;
LAUDA ANIMA; PICARDY)

Sing, Jerusalem, God's favor;
　　Shout, O Zion, God's goodwill;
Who, in time of tribulation,
　　Shall be our Defender still.
Alleluia, alleluia!
　　Let your praise God's temple fill!

God brings peace within our borders;
　　Fills our barns with finest grain;
Snow, like fleece, the fields may cover,
　　But with spring, new life they gain.
Alleluia, alleluia!
　　Faithful shall our Lord remain.

For all times God's Word is with us;
　　Ever swift the Lord's decree;
Steadfast always to the nations
　　Who to God shall faithful be.
Alleluia, alleluia!
　　Be our strength eternally.

Psalm 148

8.7.8.7.8.7 (Suggested tunes: WESTMINSTER ABBEY;
LAUDA ANIMA; PICARDY)

Praise God in the highest heaven,
    Sun and moon and stars in space;
Sing, O angels, of God's goodness;
    Tell, you ordered skies, God's grace.
Alleluia, alleluia!
    Who but God your course can trace?

All the earth will shout God's praises,
    Mountain peaks and ocean floor;
Wind and fire and beast and forest,
    Hill and desert, vale and shore.
Alleluia, alleluia!
    Honor God whom you adore.

Rise, O child of God, in wonder
    At creation's majesty;
Young and old, God's glory claiming,
    Praise the Lord in unity.
Alleluia, alleluia!
    Now and for eternity.

Psalm 149

7.7.7.7 with Alleluias (Suggested tunes: Easter Hymn; Llanfair)

Praise the Lord, new songs employ, Alleluia!
  Sing to God, who is your joy, Alleluia!
Israel, with one accord, Alleluia!
  Lift your voice unto the Lord, Alleluia!

Let your feet be still no more, Alleluia!
  Dance, your Maker to adore, Alleluia!
Strike the timbrel and the lyre, Alleluia!
  Your delight is God's desire, Alleluia!

Heirs to grace, now celebrate, Alleluia!
  God in righteousness is great, Alleluia!
Justice shall outlast our days, Alleluia!
  If we lose ourselves in praise, Alleluia!

Psalm 150

10.10.10.4 with Alleluias (Suggested tune: Sine Nomine)

Let ev'ry heart lift up God's name in praise;
Each voice a song within this temple raise
To God, whose goodness follows all our days:
Alleluia, alleluia!

The trumpet sounds the power of God's might;
The pipe and strings put all despair to flight;
And spirits dance with cymbals clear and bright:
Alleluia, alleluia!

Praise be to God in anthems strong and sure,
With bold assurance, confidence secure,
Though breath shall cease, God's love will long endure:
Alleluia, alleluia!

Index of Liturgical Use

Sunday or Festival	Year A	Year B	Year C
Advent			
First Sunday of Advent	122	80	25
Second Sunday of Advent	72	85	—
Third Sunday of Advent	146	126	—
Fourth Sunday of Advent	80	89a	80
Christmas			
Christmas Eve	96	96	96
Nativity of Jesus Christ/ Christmas Day (at dawn)	97	97	97
Nativity of Jesus Christ/ Christmas Day	98	98	98
1st Sunday after Christmas Day	148	148	148
2nd Sunday after Christmas Day	147b	147b	147b
Epiphany of the Lord or Sunday before Epiphany	72	72	72
Ordinary Time			
Baptism of the Lord	29	29	29
2nd Sunday in Ordinary Time	40	139	36
3rd Sunday in Ordinary Time	27	62	19
4th Sunday in Ordinary Time	15	111	71
5th Sunday in Ordinary Time	112	147a	138
6th Sunday in Ordinary Time	119a	30	1
7th Sunday in Ordinary Time	119b	41	37
8th Sunday in Ordinary Time	131	103	92
Transfiguration of the Lord	2, 99	50	99

Sunday or Festival	Year A	Year B	Year C
Lent			
Ash Wednesday	51	51	51
1st Sunday in Lent	32	25	91
2nd Sunday in Lent	121	22b	27
3rd Sunday in Lent	95	19	63
4th Sunday in Lent	23	107	32
5th Sunday in Lent	130	15, 119	126
Holy Week			
Passion/Palm Sunday (6th Sunday in Lent)	31b, 118	31b, 118	31b, 118
Monday of Holy Week	36	36	36
Tuesday of Holy Week	71	71	71
Wednesday of Holy Week	70	70	70
Maundy Thursday	116	116	116
Good Friday	22a	22a	22a
Easter			
Easter Vigil	16, 19, 42, 43, 46, 98, 114, 136, 143	16, 19, 42, 43, 46, 98, 114, 136, 143	16, 19, 42, 43, 46, 98, 114, 136, 143
Resurrection of the Lord/Easter	118	118	118
Easter Evening	114	114	114
2nd Sunday of Easter	16	133	118, 150
3rd Sunday of Easter	116	4	30
4th Sunday of Easter	23	23	23
5th Sunday of Easter	31a	22b	148
6th Sunday of Easter	66	98	67
Ascension of the Lord	47, 93	47, 93	47, 93
7th Sunday of Easter	68	1	97
Day of Pentecost	104b	104b	104b

Sunday or Festival	Year A	Year B	Year C
Ordinary Time			
Trinity Sunday	8	29	8
9th Sunday in Ordinary Time	46	139	96
10th Sunday in Ordinary Time	33	138	146
11th Sunday in Ordinary Time	116	20	5
12th Sunday in Ordinary Time	86	9, 133	42, 43
13th Sunday in Ordinary Time	13	130	77
14th Sunday in Ordinary Time	45b	48	30
15th Sunday in Ordinary Time	119d	24	82
16th Sunday in Ordinary Time	139	89b	52
17th Sunday in Ordinary Time	105, 128	14	85
18th Sunday in Ordinary Time	17	51	107
19th Sunday in Ordinary Time	105	130	50
20th Sunday in Ordinary Time	133	111	80
21st Sunday in Ordinary Time	124	84	71
22nd Sunday in Ordinary Time	105	45a	81
23rd Sunday in Ordinary Time	149	125	139
24th Sunday in Ordinary Time	114	19	14
25th Sunday in Ordinary Time	105	1	79
26th Sunday in Ordinary Time	78	124	91
27th Sunday in Ordinary Time	19	26	137
28th Sunday in Ordinary Time	106	22a	66a
29th Sunday in Ordinary Time	99	104a	119c
30th Sunday in Ordinary Time	90	34	65
31st Sunday in Ordinary Time	107	146	119e
All Saints' Day	34	24	149

Sunday or Festival	Year A	Year B	Year C
32nd Sunday in Ordinary Time	78	127	98, 145
33rd Sunday in Ordinary Time	123	—	—
Christ the King (or Reign of Christ)	100	132	—

CPSIA information can be obtained
at www.ICGtesting.com
Printed in the USA
FSHW020625170819
61120FS